THOMAS AQUINAS AND JOHN DUNS SCOTUS:
NATURAL THEOLOGY IN THE HIGH
MIDDLE AGES

Continuum Studies in Philosophy
Series Editor: James Fieser, University of Tennessee at Martin, USA

Continuum Studies in Philosophy is a major monograph series from Continuum. The series features first-class scholarly research monographs across the whole field of philosophy. Each work makes a major contribution to the field of philosophical research.

Aesthetic in Kant, James Kirwan
Analytic Philosophy: The History of an Illusion, Aaron Preston
Aquinas and the Ship of Theseus, Christopher Brown
Augustine and Roman Virtue, Brian Harding
The Challenge of Relativism, Patrick Phillips
Demands of Taste in Kant's Aesthetics, Brent Kalar
Descartes and the Metaphysics of Human Nature, Justin Skirry
Descartes' Theory of Ideas, David Clemenson
Dialectic of Romanticism, Peter Murphy and David Roberts
Hegel and the Analytic Tradition, edited by Angelica Nuzzo
Hegel's Philosophy of Language, Jim Vernon
Hegel's Philosophy of Right, David James
Hegel's Theory of Recognition, Sybol Cook Anderson
The History of Intentionality, Ryan Hickerson
Kierkegaard, Metaphysics and Political Theory, Alison Assiter
Kierkegaard's Analysis of Radical Evil, David A. Roberts
Leibniz Re-interpreted, Lloyd Strickland
Metaphysics and the End of Philosophy, HO Mounce
Nicholas Malebranche, Susan Peppers-Bates
Nietzsche and the Greeks, Dale Wilkerson
Origins of Analytic Philosophy, Delbert Reed
Philosophy of Miracles, David Corner
Platonism, Music and the Listener's Share, Christopher Norris
Popper's Theory of Science, Carlos Garcia
Role of God in Spinoza's Metaphysics, Sherry Deveaux
Rousseau and the Ethics of Virtue, James Delaney
Rousseau's Theory of Freedom, Matthew Simpson
Spinoza and the Stoics, Firmin DeBrabander
Spinoza's Radical Cartesian Mind, Tammy Nyden-Bullock
St. Augustine and the Theory of Just War, John Mark Mattox
St. Augustine of Hippo, R.W. Dyson
Thomas Aquinas & John Duns Scotus, Alex Hall
Tolerance and the Ethical Life, Andrew Fiala

THOMAS AQUINAS AND JOHN DUNS SCOTUS: NATURAL THEOLOGY IN THE HIGH MIDDLE AGES

Alexander W. Hall

continuum

Continuum

The Tower Building
11 York Road
London
SE1 7NX

80 Maiden Lane
Suite 704
New York
NY 10038

www.continuumbooks.com

British Library Cataloguing-in-Publication Data
A catalogue record for this book is available from the British Library.

ISBN: PB: 978-1-4411-8408-5

Library of Congress Cataloging-in-Publication Data
A catalog record for this book is available from the Library of Congress.

Typeset by Fakenham Photosetting, Fakenham, Norfolk

For my Wife Tuyet, my children Maia and Dylan,
and my parents Terrence and Donna Hall

Contents

Acknowledgements   ix
Preface   xi
List of Abbreviations   xiii
List of Translations   xv

1   Natural Theology in the High Middle Ages   1
2   Aquinas and *Scientia*   28
3   *Scientia, Analogia,* and the Five Ways   49
4   Scotus and *Scientia*   75
5   Scotus on Naming and Understanding   86
6   Scotus on the Signification of Theological Discourse   101
7   Infinitude, Transcendental Signification and Analogy   110

Sources Consulted   121
Notes   131
Index   167

Acknowledgements

Material from *John Duns Scotus, Philosophical Writings*, translated with introduction and notes by Allan Wolter (Indianapolis: Hackett, 1987); and from 'Summa theologiae,' in *Basic Writings of Saint Thomas Aquinas*, edited and annotated, with an introduction, by Anton C. Pegis, 2 vols. (New York: Random House, 1944) is reprinted by permission of Hackett Publishing Company, Inc. All rights reserved. Material from *John Duns Scotus, God and Creatures: The Quodlibetal Questions*, translated with introduction, notes, and glossary by Felix Alluntis and Allan B. Wolter (Princeton, NJ: Princeton University Press, 1975) is used with permission of The Catholic University of America Press, Washington, D.C. Material from John Duns Scotus, *Opera omnia*, edited by C. Balić, et al. Vatican Scotistic Commission (Rome: Polyglot Press, 1950–) is used with permission of Commissione Internazionale Scotista critica della *Opera omnia* del Beato Giovanni Duns Scoto.

Preface

This book began as a dissertation written at Emory University under Jack Zupko, whose wisdom and mentorship inspire my work as a scholar and educator. I also owe thanks to Gyula Klima for encouragement and advice at the outset of this project, as well as to numerous scholars who shared their expertise with me at the sessions of various learned societies, and to Lloyd Newton who allowed me the use of his forthcoming edition of Scotus's *Quaestiones in librum Praedicamentorum*. In addition I am deeply grateful to Richard Berquist for generously sharing with me his considerable knowledge concerning ancient and medieval conceptions of *scientia*. Where the sound advice of these scholars has not been incorporated into the final product, it is generally because a recommendation came too late to see print. This especially concerns the advice given me in response to a presentation of my research at an annual meeting of the International Duns Scotus Society where Timothy Noone and Stephen Dumont, respectively, noted work to be done as concerns both the meaning of Scotus's assertion that our knowledge of God is confused and his rejection of prior and posterior signification. I am also grateful to the two additional members of my dissertation committee, Thomas Flynn and Steven Strange; my readers Pamela Hall and Mark Risjord; and to John Glanville and Armand Fernandez, teachers who inspired my love of philosophy. Of course the views expressed in this book are my own and may not be shared by those who helped me. Finally, heartfelt thanks goes to my wife Tuyet whose considerable sacrifice and support made this work possible.

List of Abbreviations

An	Aristotle, *On the Soul*
An.Post	Aristotle, *Posterior Analytics*
CHLMP	Norman Kretzmann et al. (eds), *The Cambridge History of Later Medieval Philosophy*
De Div. Nom	Dionysius, *De divinus nominibus*
De primo princ.	Scotus, *On the First Principle*
In DA	Aquinas, *Sententia super De anima*
In PA	Aquinas, *Sententia super Posteriora analytica*
Met	Aristotle, *Metaphysics*
NAB	New American Bible
Ord.	Scotus, *Ordinatio*
Quodl.	Scotus, *Quaestiones quodlibetales*
SCG	Aquinas, *Summa contra gentiles*
ST	Aquinas, *Summa theologiae*

List of Translations

An.Post (from the Greek): Translated by Jonathan Barnes, in: Aristotle. *The Complete Works of Aristotle: The Revised Oxford Translation.* Edited by J. Barnes. 2 vols. Bollingen Series. Princeton: Princeton University Press, 1984.

An.Post (from the Latin): Translated by F. R. Larcher, in: Thomas Aquinas. *Commentary on the 'Posterior Analytics' of Aristotle.* Preface by James A. Weisheipl. New York: Magi Books, 1970.

De primo princ: Translated by Allan B. Wolter, in: John Duns Scotus. *A Treatise on God as First Principle.* Chicago: Franciscan Herald Press, 1966.

In PA: Larcher.

De Interpretatione: Translated by J. L. Ackrill, in: Barnes, ed., vol. 1.

Met (from the Greek): Translated by W. D. Ross, in: Barnes, ed., vol. 2.

Met (from the Latin): Rowan.

Ord: Translated by Allan Wolter, in: *Philosophical Writings: A Selection.* With introduction and notes by Allan Wolter. Cambridge: Hackett Publishing Company, 1987.

Ord: Translated by William A. Frank and Allan B. Wolter, in: *Duns Scotus, Metaphysician.* West Lafayette, IN: Purdue University Press, 1995.

Quodl: Translated by Felix Alluntis and Allan B. Wolter, in: *John Duns Scotus, God and Creatures: The Quodlibetal Questions.* Introduction, notes, and glossary by Felix Alluntis and Allan B. Wolter. Princeton, NJ: Princeton University Press, 1975.

Republic: Translated by Paul Shorey, in *Plato: The Collected Dialogues.* Edited by Edith Hamilton and Huntington Cairns. Princeton: Princeton University Press, 1961.

SCG: Translated by Anton C. Pegis, et al. Notre Dame: University of Notre Dame Press, 1975.

In DA: Translated by Kenelm Foster and Silvester Humphries, in: *Commentary on Aristotle's 'De Anima.'* Introduction by Ralph McInerny. Notre Dame: Dumb Ox Books, 1994.

Sententia super Metaphysiciam: Translated by John Rowan, in: *Commentary on Aristotle's 'Metaphysics.'* Introduction by John Rowan, preface by Ralph McInerny. Notre Dame: Dumb Ox Books, 1995.

ST: Translated by Fathers of the English Dominican Province, in: *Basic Writings of Saint Thomas Aquinas.* Edited and annotated, with an introduction, by Anton C. Pegis. 2 vols. New York: Random House, 1944

Unless otherwise noted, I rely solely on these translations. I use two translations of the *Ordinatio,* providing the English title in the citation. It is sometimes difficult to correlate a passage from these translations back to the Latin critical edition, so I also provide the page numbers from the English edition. For example '*Ord.* I, d. 3, q. 1, n. 26, *Duns Scotus, Metaphysician,* 109' refers to p. 109 of *Duns Scotus, Metaphysician.* Citations from *Ord.* I, d. 22, q. un., Appendix A provide page numbers from the Vatican edition as the editors do not organize this material into numbered sections. On occasion, I tacitly introduce minor modifications in the interest of preserving consistency.

Chapter 1

Natural Theology in the High Middle Ages

The High Middle Ages occupies a space of relative calm that began after two centuries of unrest following Charlemagne's death in 814, and ended in the warfare and plague of the fourteenth century. During this period Catholic Europe enjoyed a cultural flourishing and scholastic philosophy reached the height of its influence, generally in the hands of professional theologians who lived and worked in England and parts of Europe in the great universities of the day.[1] Emerging from the Carolingian revival, scholastic philosophy appraised the Greco-Roman, Arabic, and Jewish philosophical traditions from a Christian standpoint, and scholastic thinkers in general appreciated the achievements of their pagan predecessors, even crediting them with some grasp of the divine:

> There are some truths which the natural reason also is able to reach. Such are that God exists, that he is one, and the like. In fact, such truths about God have been proved demonstratively by the philosophers,[2] guided by the light of the natural reason. (SCG I.3.2)

However, the schoolmen also maintain that without revelation it is extremely difficult to attain spiritually significant insight:

> If the only way open to us for the knowledge of God were solely that of reason, the human race would remain in the blackest shadows of ignorance. For the knowledge of God, which especially renders men perfect and good, would come to be possessed only by a few, and these few would require a great deal of time in order to reach it. (SCG I.4.5)

Nonetheless medieval Christian thinkers help themselves to the fruits of prior research in logic, ethics, semiotics, epistemology, and metaphysics, though not all were equally comfortable with the integration of non-Christian thinkers, and even those who advocated an active engagement with the philosophical tradition approached the task with caution.

One reason for this hesitation was the Platonic strain in medieval philosophy. Though their direct access to Plato was for all intents limited to a translation of the first part of his *Timaeus*,[3] Plato's interest in the transcendent at the expense of the mundane stamped itself on the medieval mind through the influence of thinkers such as Augustine. In the spirit of Plato's claim that the body is a tomb,[4] medievals referred to themselves as 'wayfarers (*viatores*),' and this devaluation of sublunary existence coupled with a mistrust of the human intellect led some such as the Parisian theologian Henry of Ghent to claim that no certainty is attainable without divine assistance in the form of a direct illumination from God.[5]

A more empirical outlook gathered supporters in the twelfth and thirteenth centuries with the reintroduction of Aristotle to the Latin West. Before the twelfth century, European thinkers had only a few of Aristotle's writings in translation. Christendom's contact with the East changed this. Arabic philosophers had studied Aristotle for generations and in the twelfth century their interest communicated itself to the schoolmen. By the mid-thirteenth century translators working mainly in Spain and Sicily had rendered almost the entire Aristotelian corpus as it is known today into Latin.[6] The reintroduction of Aristotle had a seismic impact on medieval Europe. The *Trivium* of grammar, rhetoric, and logic along with the *Quadrivium* of arithmetic, geometry, music, and astronomy were gradually either replaced by or adapted to Aristotle's writings, and the empirical bent of his philosophy inspired natural theologians who worked to demonstrate the truth of revelation without reliance on premises taken from Scripture. These thinkers favored a cautious integration of Aristotle's thought, and despite injunctions against lecturing on Aristotle,[7] eventually had their way.

Behind the reluctance to embrace Aristotle was the justified fear that his pagan philosophical worldview is irreconcilable with Christianity. Aristotle believes the world to be eternal[8] rather than created, and his discussion of human souls appears to discount the possibility of personal immortality.[9] It is no wonder that Christian thinkers approached his thought with circumspection.

*

Writing at the University of Paris around 1270, Thomas Aquinas (who joined the Dominican Order at the age of eighteen against the wishes of his wealthy Italian family) offered demonstrations of God's existence and other truths about the divine essence without recourse to revelation. Aquinas does not discount revelation, but believes that some of its insights are verifiable (and have been verified) by independent means.[10] His project is inspired by Aristotle's empiricist outlook, but Aquinas urges caution. He believes that the articles of faith (and positions that contradict them) cannot be proven through valid demonstrative arguments (ST Ia.46.2; SCG II.32). Positions that oppose faith are indemonstrable because both reason and revelation have their source in God. Hence, 'whatever arguments are brought forward against the doctrines of faith are conclusions incorrectly derived from the first and self-evident principles imbedded in nature' (SCG I.7.7). Aquinas's insistence on this principle aids his effort to 'baptize' Aristotle, but Aquinas is performing a balancing act. As a natural theologian he believes that Aristotelian empiricism can clarify our picture of the divine nature, and he is encouraged by Aristotle's ability to progress as far as he did without the benefit of revelation, yet as a Christian intellectual he senses a danger in Aristotle's approach. Moreover, Aristotle's writings had been used to support propositions that directly contradict revelation, and in the arts faculty, where the focus was on Aristotelian philosophy rather than theology, masters such as Siger of Brabant were arguing that these propositions were true.[11] Ultimately Siger's ideas precipitated a backlash from the Church in the form of the Condemnation of 1277, which Aquinas (who died in 1274) did not live to see. The other difficulty in adapting Aristotle's methods lay in Aquinas's conception of God as a being radically different from anything encountered in this world, for this suggests that empiricist approaches may be unable to adduce evidence in support of propositions concerning the divine essence.

Writing some thirty years after Aquinas, John Duns Scotus, a Franciscan of Scottish descent who was educated in England and lectured in Oxford, Paris, Cologne, and possibly Cambridge, shared Aquinas's conviction that the power of reason is sufficient unto itself to attain knowledge of God through a study of creation, and like Aquinas, Scotus met with opposition. But while Aquinas was concerned to show that Aristotelian empiricism need not put reason at odds with revelation, Scotus had to reckon with thinkers who looked to a more Augustinian approach following the Condemnation of 1277. Specifically, Scotus contended with the followers of the influential Parisian schoolman and secular priest Henry of Ghent, who drew from Augustine to support the claim that human reason is powerless to confirm the truths of Scripture without assistance from God in the form of a divine illumination.[12]

Shortly after Aquinas's death and around twenty-eight years before Scotus incepted as a master of theology, then bishop of Paris Stephen Tempier drafted the aforementioned Condemnation of 219 articles in theology and natural philosophy under the direction of Pope John XXI. The Condemnation had the effect of emphasizing God's omnipotence while discrediting the autonomy of reason[13] and thus striking a blow to the empiricist tradition.[14] The Condemnation was primarily targeted against Siger of Brabant and his followers, who supported a group of ideas known collectively as Latin Averroism,[15] after the Islamic philosopher Ibn Rushd whose Latinized name was Averroes. Siger maintained that though God exists, he is unaware of anything other than himself; there is no providence; the existence of the world is owing to the necessary activity of agencies intermediate between God and creation; there is no personal immortality; and human wills are not free, but rather ruled by the movements of the planets.[16] In 1270, these claims brought Siger into conflict with the Church, when the bishop of Paris condemned a list of thirteen propositions drawn from Siger's writings.[17] Finally, Siger's teachings precipitated the Condemnation of 1277, where he was charged with the heresy of maintaining the truth of philosophical principles that opposed Christian faith. Siger repudiated this position, allowing that only doctrines of faith are strictly speaking true, yet went on to defend the right of philosophers to reason freely. The claim that philosophy and religion can generate conflicting truths has come to be known as the theory of two truths; and as this theory was linked to Aristotle, the Condemnation cast disrepute on thinkers such as Aquinas,[18] who in actuality had labored to refute Siger and his circle.

Wary of the reading of Aristotle developing among the arts faculty, Aquinas—whose staggering workload may have contributed to his death at the age of forty-nine[19]—wrote a series of detailed commentaries on the works of Aristotle, perhaps with the aim of rescuing Aristotle from the arts masters and defending his own project of adapting Aristotle's empiricist standpoint to the task of natural theology.[20] The initial results of Aquinas's work were not promising. Included in the Condemnation of 1277 were nineteen propositions taken from his writings.[21]

*

The Condemnation, which Henry of Ghent had a hand in drafting, brought about a short-lived Augustinian revival in which the doctrine of illumination took center stage at the University of Paris.[22] The danger of this doctrine in the eyes of Aquinas and Scotus is that it degrades human beings and (at least for Aquinas) by implication the creator.[23] Moreover, the teaching that an illumination is required in order to know God is against Scripture, which states, 'Since the creation of the world, invisible realities, God's eternal power and divinity, have become visible, recognized through the things he has made' (Rom. 1.20 NAB).[24] Like Aquinas, Scotus was attracted to an empirical approach, and like Aquinas he expressed doubts about the reliability of the knowledge that such investigations yield.[25] However, unlike Aquinas, whose alternative to illuminationism met with initial hostility thanks to disrepute cast on Aristotelian natural theology by Siger and his followers,[26] Scotus's attack on the doctrine succeeded, and by the time of Scotus's death in Cologne in 1308, around the age of forty-three, the doctrine of illumination had ceased to be a serious contender in scholastic efforts to ascertain the epistemic warrant for claims of certitude.[27]

Scotus's critique of the doctrine of illumination together with his insistence that God enables us to learn of him through creation lends dignity to reason, yet Scotus faced difficulties similar to those that caused Aquinas to pause when weighing the benefits of Aristotelian empiricism. Our knowledge of the divine essence is mediated and hence incomplete:

> I affirm that by their natural powers neither an angel nor the soul in any of its states can have mediate knowledge of the divine essence in all its proper meaning, so that the sense or meaning of that essence would be grasped in knowing or by knowing some intermediary object. (*Quodl.* 14.74)

Scotus's sentiment does not entail apophaticism, but it seems to challenge our ability to form an accurate picture of God's essence by studying the qualities of creatures. As Scotus notes, God's 'pure perfection ... is repugnant ... to the entire category of quality and to the whole class of things that are caused' (*Quodl.* 3.53). Before considering what Scotus believes we can learn of God's nature, let us look back some thirty years and see how these issues played out in Aquinas's writings, the reason for the comparison being that despite their agreement that the distance between creator and creation challenges our efforts to learn of the former via the latter, the two are sometimes construed as having arrived at quite divergent conclusions regarding what we can know about God.[28]

*

Aquinas's project of applying Aristotelian empiricism to the task of natural theology was nearly derailed by Siger and the Latin Averroists. Natural theology, defined as the attempt to confirm revelation without recourse to Scripture or the supernatural, relies on reason's inability validly to contradict faith. Aware of the controversy fermenting in the arts faculty and that his optimistic views about the power of unaided reason were not universally endorsed, Aquinas's discussions of the intellect's capabilities with respect to the discernment of characteristics proper to the divine essence are cautious. As noted, he allows that in some cases the best one can hope for is to show the falsity of a proposition that opposes faith (ST Ia.46.2; SCG II.32), and he allows that we are unable in this life to attain knowledge of God's essence save through an act of grace (ST Ia.12.4c). What we can learn of God is abstractive, incomplete, and confused, and theological discourse is at best analogical, meaning that when a term is said of both God and creatures we must allow that the idea of God that it brings to mind is imperfect, though not uninformative (SCG I.32, 34; ST Ia.13.5c).

By contrast Scotus's claim that theological discourse is univocal or significative of ideas that refer to God and creatures without any shift in meaning whatsoever (e.g., *Ord.* I, d. 3, q. 2, n. 26) appears brash, especially for one writing *after* the Condemnation of 1277. In response, we may note that one concept can subsume multiple entities without uniquely referring to any one particular entity, as the concept of animal subsumes a host of different species. Along these lines, Scotus appears to allow for a sense of univocity where one word can conceive one idea that subsumes both God and creatures without holding that this concept is any more an accurate representation of the divine essence than the concept of a human as nothing more than an animal accurately reflects what it is to be human (cf., *Ord.* I, d. 22, q. un.; *Quodl.* 14.13). This understanding of univocity reflects Scotus's awareness of the epistemic gap between creator and creation owing to the necessarily mediated status of our knowledge of the divine essence, which Scotus illustrates with the example of the intellection of the redness of an unseen piece of glass, whose color is glimpsed only in the light that filters through it:

> An example from sense perception makes this clear. When a ray of light passes through a piece of red glass, it causes red to appear on the opposite wall. Now the red on the wall is not a means for seeing the red of the glass properly, but one sees the red of the glass only in a derivative sense or perhaps not at all,

for there is only some similarity between the red on the wall and
that of the glass. (*Quodl.* 14.88)

So too, Scotus believes our knowledge of God to be mediated and
imperfect; the question is to what extent he acknowledges that
conceptions proper (i.e., uniquely referring) to God's essence are
accurate.

These interpretations of Scotus and Aquinas revolve around
their ideas about meaning and reference. Like all schoolmen, their
semiotics develop from a passage in Aristotle's *De Interpretatione*:
'Spoken sounds are symbols of affections in the soul' (1, 16ª4–6).[29]
The medievals believed that the world is cognitively present via the
medium of ideas,[30] but they differed over whether words refer to
ideas or directly to things in the world inasmuch as these things
are cognitively present.[31] The former interpretation, described
by Scotus as the *prima via* (first way), constitutes the traditional
medieval understanding of signification: words bring to mind (or
signify) ideas, which in turn are signs of things. Scotus notes several
difficulties with this position. For instance, 'Socrates exists' and
other existential propositions would always be true if words signify
ideas. Provided one has an idea of Socrates and the term 'Socrates'
signifies only that idea, for as long as one has the idea it will be true
that Socrates (that is the idea of Socrates) exists. In place of this
paradigm, Scotus adopts the second way (*secunda via*), which holds
that words directly signify things rather than ideas.[32] Contrast this
with Aquinas who affirms:

This term 'man' signifies human nature in abstraction from
singulars. Thus it is impossible that it should immediately signify
a single man. Whence the Platonists supposed that it signified the
very idea of man [as a] separate [entity]. But because, according
to Aristotle, this [sentiment] concerning an idea's separation[33]
does not stand up, but rather the idea exists only in the intellect,
it was necessary for Aristotle to claim that words immediately
signify conceptions of the intellect and by mediation of these
[conceptions words signify] things. (*Expositio libri Peryermenias*, I,
1.2, n. 15, trans. mine)[34]

Scotus too denies that terms refer to Platonic ideas, defined as universals possessed of eternal existence apart from the particular entities that imperfectly instantiate (or copy) them, which particulars are what they are (or are real) only inasmuch as they are accurate copies of these ideas.[35] Instead, as regards extramental entities he believes that words signify these entities insofar as they are cognitively present to us through our ideas, thus words do not signify things as they exist but rather as they are 'perceived by the intellect.'[36]

Scotus and Aquinas agree that ideas are ultimately traceable to things in the world and this raises a difficulty. In this life we do not directly experience God, who is radically different from creation, so from where do we get our ideas of God's essence and how do we know that they are accurate? The doctrine of illumination sidesteps these difficulties: we know of God through a direct illumination given to us by him.[37] We can begin discussing how Aquinas and Scotus respond to this challenge by considering the conception of God's nature shared by most schoolmen, who believe that God created the entire universe from nothing, and that God's power is ultimately responsible for the coming into existence and passing away of all things. God himself, of course, is uncreated. Since his existence is uncaused, medieval thinkers claim that God exists because of what he is, or through his essence. Put another way, God's existence is necessary. As a corollary, God is utterly simple. All other entities are something other than bare existence. For each there is a reason that it exists in a particular manner at a particular time, for nothing happens without a cause. But there must be some exception to this rule or we will never arrive at an entity capable of accounting for all others, for the activity of every entity would require a cause, leading to an infinite regress. God is this exception, and as pure being he exists unqualifiedly. To say, for instance, that God is good is to assert that God exists in a particular manner and we would require an explanation why God exists in this manner and not some other, returning us to an infinite regress. Hence God's attributes are identified with his essence, which is simply to be. Accordingly God revealed himself to Moses as 'I am who am' (Exod. 3.14 NAB).

Medieval theologians generally agree that we cannot comprehend how God possesses every perfection while remaining simple.[38] As Aquinas phrases the difficulty: 'It seems that the perfections of all things are not in God. For God is simple ... whereas the perfections of things are many and diverse' (ST Ia.4.2, arg. 1). Aquinas navigates this epistemic gap with the belief that effects resemble their causes, as the warmth of a kettle resembles the heat of the fire. God is known through creation and our best qualities reveal something of his essence: 'Let us make man in our image, after our likeness' (Gen. 1.26 NAB) (cf., SCG I.29.3).

Medievals trace the lineage of the distinction between things as they are understood and things as they actually exist in a realm beyond our own to Plato. According to the common medieval understanding of Plato, for almost every type of thing in the world, there exists an eternal pattern or exemplar, the aforementioned ideas or forms.[39] This eternal exemplar is the unique and perfect instance of the particulars patterned after it, which owe their existence as particular kinds of things to the forms they imperfectly instantiate or copy. In the world there exists a multitude of human beings, while in the realm of the forms there exists only the form of humanity: perfect, unique, eternal, and that by which any human is human. Platonism entered Christianity through several channels, one particularly influential source being Pseudo-Dionysius the Areopagite, mistakenly thought by the medievals to be the same Dionysius who sat with the Athenian council on the hill of Ares (the Areopagus) to appraise the merits of Christianity as argued by St. Paul, and who forthwith became the latter's disciple (Acts, 17.22–34).[40] Aquinas cites Dionysius when discussing the accuracy of our knowledge of God:

> Some of the ... names [said of God] signify a perfection without defect. This is true with reference to that which the name was imposed to signify; for as to the mode of signification, every name is defective. For by means of a name we express things in the way in which the intellect conceives them. For our intellect, taking the origin of its knowledge from the senses, does not transcend the mode which is found in sensible things, in which

the form and the subject of the form are not identical owing to the composition of form and matter ... As a result, with reference to the mode of signification there is in every name that we use an imperfection, which does not befit God, even though the thing signified in some eminent way does befit God ... And so with reference to the mode of signification no name is fittingly applied to God; this is done only with reference to that which the name has been imposed to signify. Such names, therefore, as Dionysius teaches, [*De divinis nominibus*, I, 5 (*De Div. Nom.*); *De caelesti hierarchia*, II, 3] can be both affirmed and denied of God. They can be affirmed because of the meaning of the name; they can be denied because of the mode of signification. (SCG I.30.3, brackets mine)

We impose names to refer to entities that are not wholly identical with their attributes. This poses a difficulty when we refer to God ideas that are bound up with defects unbefitting divine simplicity. Still, attributes such as goodness and wisdom are ultimately traceable to God and, as effects, bear some relation to their cause. It is thus permissible to affirm that God is good, wise, etc., provided we acknowledge that our ordinary way or mode of signification is bound up with notions of finitude unbefitting the divine essence and hence cannot afford a perfectly accurate conception of his nature. Still, there is more involved in referring our ideas to God than simply removing the connotation of creaturely imperfections.

Dionysius believes that terms appropriately said of God not only lack any connotation of finitude or imperfection but also bring to mind God's supereminence,[41] and Aquinas agrees, noting in the passage under consideration that 'the thing signified in some eminent way does befit God' (SCG I.30.3). He continues by linking God's eminence (or supereminence) to negative theology, which denies positive knowledge of God's essence: 'The mode of supereminence in which the abovementioned perfections are found in God can be signified by names used by us only through negation, as when we say that God is eternal or infinite' (SCG I.30.4). With respect to his assertion that God is infinite, Aquinas elsewhere notes that this means that 'there is no terminus or limit to his

perfection' (SCG I.43.3).[42] Therefore, 'there cannot be a mode
of perfection, nor is one thinkable, by which a given perfection is
possessed more fully than it is possessed by the being that is perfect
through its essence' (SCG I.43.9). This provides a more positive
account of our knowledge of God, characterizing his perfections
in terms of infinite being. In this passage Aquinas does not clarify
what it means to possess a perfection most fully, but elsewhere he
discusses this in terms of God's pure actuality, negatively definable
as the lack of potentiality to undergo alteration.[43] Thus at least a
part of the explanation for Aquinas's assertion that God possesses
his perfections most fully is that they cannot be divorced from his
essence. From considerations relating to potentiality, we may add
two further consequences of God's pure actuality: (1) God has
every perfection (were any lacking God would stand in potentiality
to their reception) (ST Ia.4.1c; SCG I.28),[44] and (2) God is wholly
identical with his perfections (as all composition entails potentiality) (SCG I.18.31).

Aquinas's aforementioned claim that the divine names apply
only through negation suggests that we lack any positive knowledge
of God's essence.[45] As he notes:

> The mode of supereminence in which the abovementioned
> perfections are found in God can be signified by names used
> by us only through negation, as when we say that God is eternal
> or infinite, or also through a relation of God to other things,
> as when he is called the first cause or the highest good. For we
> cannot grasp what God is, but only what he is not and how other
> things are related to him. (SCG I.30.4)[46]

Again, Aquinas notes that God has no name because we cannot
understand God's essence (ST Ia.13.1, ad 1). Nonetheless, Aquinas
insists our knowledge of God is not purely negative; such a way of
thinking 'is against the intention of those who speak of God. For in
saying that God lives, they assuredly mean more than to say that ...
he differs from inanimate bodies' (ST Ia.13.2c). Thus, 'it does not
follow that God is good because he causes goodness; but rather ...
he causes goodness in things because he is good' (ibid.).

Aquinas is balancing the demands of Aristotelian natural theology against an inherited Platonic conception of God's essence. Consider the resemblance between his understanding of the divine perfections and Plato's theory of forms. Both the forms and the divine attributes are unique archetypical realities somehow responsible for the existence of the particulars that imitate them to one degree or another. Yet Aquinas, along with medieval thinkers in general, adapts Plato's system to Christian ends. While Plato appears to believe in a multitude of individual forms, Christian thinkers placed every perfection in God and identified them with his essence. God is goodness itself and responsible for all goodness in creation, and likewise wisdom itself, etc. Aquinas acknowledges that our concepts of God are imperfect representations, but views this as unavoidable. Goodness belongs to the divine nature and yet God is goodness itself. We might look on God's goodness as a facet of his essence but this is inaccurate. A facet is an aspect and thus other than the whole, whereas God is completely each of his attributes, the sum of which constitutes an utterly simple essence. Valid arguments have led reason to posit the existence of a being whose nature we cannot comprehend. As creator, God must be utterly simple; this entails a unity in multiplicity that we cannot grasp, yet if theological discourse is meaningful the isolated perfections it considers must belong to God. As Scotus points out, if words said of God take on wholly unrelated meanings there is no more reason to affirm goodness of God than there is to claim that God is a rock (*Ord.* I, d. 3, n. 40).

*

Owing to the distance between creator and creation, words fittingly attributed to God take on new meanings that are related to but distinct from those they possess when used to speak of creatures. Technically, one term with multiple significates is equivocal, having different meanings when used in different contexts. Thus 'bat' has numerous unrelated meanings: (1) wooden club, (2) nocturnal mammal, (3) to wink, etc. Aquinas does not allow that terms said of God and creatures are unrelated in this manner. If words such as 'good' take on a wholly new meaning when applied to God, theology is an exercise in futility. Rather Aquinas believes that terms predicated of God are fittingly applied inasmuch as the attributes they bring to mind truly characterize the divine essence, though their creaturely mode of signification is defective. To clarify the various types of signification at work in theological discourse, Aquinas turns to the tradition surrounding analogy. Following Boethius's sixth-century commentary on Aristotle's *Categories*, the schoolmen call a term that has multiple related significates 'equivocal by design (*aequivoca a consilio*),' or 'analogical.' Aquinas uses different types of analogy at different points in his career,[47] yet seems to settle on analogy of one-to-another (*unum habet proportionem ad alterum*), also called 'analogy of attribution,') designed to name things that are related to one another as cause to effect (SCG I.34; ST Ia.13.5). Sometimes these analogical terms apply primarily to the cause (that is on hearing the term we are apt to conceive the cause), as 'being' applies primarily to substances and secondarily to accidents. In these cases 'the same thing is found to be prior both according to the meaning of the name and according to the nature of the thing' (SCG I.34.5). In other instances, these analogical terms apply primarily to the effect and only derivatively to the cause, as 'healthy' applies primarily to the health of an individual and secondarily to medicine, though the latter is the cause of the former. When this transpires the order according to the meaning of the name and according to the nature of what is signified is reversed, as is the case when terms primarily significative of creatures are used to speak of God:

> Thus, therefore, because we come to a knowledge of God from other things, the reality in the names said of God and other things belongs by priority in God according to his mode of being, but the meaning of the name belongs to God by posteriority. And so he is said to be named from his effects. (SCG I.34.6)

That is, while God is the cause in creatures of what we attribute to him, when we ascribe some characteristic to God our notion is rooted in experience. This is why such analogical terms import an imperfection in the mode of signification with respect to the divine essence.[48]

This connection between signification and God's causal activity perhaps led the celebrated Thomist Etienne Gilson to claim, 'God is not more good, just, wise, powerful than the healing remedy is healthy. Nevertheless, what we call goodness, justice, wisdom, power is certainly in God since God is its cause.' [49] These comments seem to emphasize what Gilson calls the 'agnostic' interpretation of Aquinas,[50] but Aquinas's discussion of analogy of attribution in relation to competing theories of predication presents a different picture:

> [Concerning God's names] some have said that [they] ... have been brought into use more to remove something from God than to posit something in him. Hence they assert that when we say that God lives, we mean that God is not like an inanimate thing[51] ... Others[52] say that these names applied to God signify his relationship towards creatures: thus in the words, 'God is good', we mean, God is the cause of goodness in things ... Both of these opinions ... seem to be untrue ... First because in neither ... can a reason be assigned why some names more than others should be applied to God. For he is assuredly the cause of bodies in the same way as he is the cause of good things ... Secondly, because ... all names applied to God would be said of him ... in a secondary sense, as healthy is secondarily said of medicine, because it signifies only the cause of health in the animal which primarily is called healthy.[53] Thirdly, because this is against the intention of those who speak of God. For in saying that God lives, they assuredly mean more than to say that he is the cause of our life or that he differs from inanimate bodies ... Therefore we must hold a different doctrine ... God prepossesses in himself all the perfections of creatures [cf., ST Ia.4.2] ... Hence every creature represents him ... as the excelling source of whose form the effects fall short, although they derive some kind of likeness thereto [cf., ST Ia.4.3] ... Therefore, the aforesaid names signify the divine substance, but in an imperfect manner, even as creatures represent it imperfectly. So, when we say, 'God

is good', the meaning is not, 'God is the cause of goodness', or, 'God is not evil'; but ... 'Whatever good we attribute to creatures, pre-exists in God', and in a higher way. Hence it does not follow that God is good, because he causes goodness; but rather on the contrary, he causes goodness in things because he is good. (ST Ia.13.2c, brackets mine)

Aquinas is clear that theological discourse supposes more than God's being the cause of creaturely perfections. This echoes an earlier claim in the same work:

Everything can be called good and a being inasmuch as it participates in the first being by way of a certain assimilation, although distantly and defectively ... Everything is therefore called good from divine goodness, as from the first exemplary, effective and final principle of all goodness. Nevertheless everything is called good by reason of the likeness of the divine goodness belonging to it, which is formally its own goodness, whereby it is denominated good. (ST Ia.6.4c)[54]

In sum, though Aquinas exhibits apophatic tendencies and suggests that theological discourse signifies God merely as the cause of certain perfections, he is nonetheless clear that God is characterizable in terms of the best traits to be found in creatures and his comments about supereminence can help us discover how these characteristics are to be attributed to the divine essence. Moreover, passages that suggest apophatic or agnostic tendencies should be read in light of Aquinas's criticisms of both approaches.

*

Writing some thirty years after Aquinas, Scotus claims that words spoken of God and creatures can be univocal, meaning that their significates refer equally to both:

I say that God is conceived not only in a concept analogous to the concept of a creature, that is, one which is wholly other than that which is predicated of creatures, but even in some concept univocal to himself and to a creature. (*Ord.* I, d. 3, q. 1, n. 26, *Duns Scotus, Metaphysician,* 109)

This is followed with Scotus's definition of what it means for a term to be univocal:

And lest there be a dispute about the name 'univocation,' I designate that concept univocal which possesses sufficient unity in itself, so that to affirm and deny it of one and the same thing would be a contradiction. It also has sufficient unity to serve as the middle term of a syllogism, so that wherever two extremes are united by a middle term that is one in this way, we may conclude to the union of the two extremes among themselves. (Ibid.)

Scotus's comment about the uselessness of analogical predication[55] taken with his claim that we possess concepts univocal to God and creatures appears to put him at odds with Aquinas, who believes that terms said of God and creatures are analogical, and denies that we possess concepts univocal to God and creatures (ST Ia.13.5). Yet this picture is inaccurate; the theory of analogy that Scotus is most interested in debunking is Henry of Ghent's, not Aquinas's, and Scotus's and Aquinas's understandings of the signification of theological discourse coincide on several key points. Though Scotus allows that we conceive God and creatures via univocal (or univocating)[56] terms, he shares Aquinas's belief that God is simple. Thus Scotus could not maintain that our concepts of God's attributes and perfections perfectly represent the divine essence, for our concepts are concepts of isolated characteristics which must exist unitedly in God. Our finite minds cannot properly account for God's unity in diversity. Instead Scotus claims that our understanding of God dimly mirrors his essence (*Quodl.* 14.89).

Henry of Ghent received the degree of Doctor of Theology in 1277, three years after the deaths of Aquinas and Bonaventure, when Scotus himself was about ten years old. Henry's star never shone as brightly as theirs, yet he was a highly influential thinker at the University of Paris, called by Bishop Stephen Tempier to

serve on the commission that drew up the Condemnation of
1277, and again by Pope Martin IV to arbitrate the dispute over
whether mendicant friars could hear confessions.[57] When Scotus
began his theological studies at Oxford, sometime around 1278,
Henry's views were well known and defended by a number of
Franciscans,[58] and it is against Henry, not Aquinas, that Scotus
launches the bulk of his criticism of analogy.[59] Indeed, when
Scotus's criticisms began to circulate, thinkers such as Richard of
Conington, a master at Oxford in 1305, saw them for what they
were, viz., attacks targeted at Henry, and sought to refute them
as such.[60]

Scotus takes Henry to believe that God is so unlike creatures
that knowledge of the divine essence requires direct illumination.
To the extent that Henry holds this position he is inspired by
Augustine, who in his *De Trinitate* discusses how we form concepts
that pertain to God, as for example our notion of divine goodness.
Augustine's instruction is to reflect on '"this good" and "that
good"; [then] take away "this" and "that," and see good itself if you
can; so you will see God who is good not by another good, but is
the good of every good' (8.3, quoted in *Duns Scotus, Metaphysician*,
138, brackets mine). The phrase 'if you can' points to the need for
illumination, which Augustine raises at the end of this passage: 'In
all these good things ... we would be unable to call one better than
the other ... if the idea of the good itself had not been impressed
upon us' (ibid.). As a result of this process of reflection and illumination, Henry thinks we possess two distinct though related ideas
that are signified by one word, which he calls analogical.[61]

Scotus's objections point out that Henry's theory renders both
God and creatures unknowable. First, were the human mind so
weak as to require an illumination to know God, it would not be
able to hold knowledge thus acquired:

No certitude is possible where something incompatible with
certitude concurs. For just as we can infer only a contingent
proposition from a necessary and a contingent proposition
combined, so also a concurrence of what is certain [viz., illumi-
nation] and what is uncertain [viz., a human mind] does not

produce certain knowledge. (*Ord.* I, d. 3, pars 1, q. 4, n. 221, *Philosophical Writings*, 104, brackets mine)

So we would not be capable of retaining knowledge about God acquired through illuminations. On the other hand, proponents of illumination maintain that the world is in continual flux while illuminations are supposed to reveal timeless truths, but:

> If an object is continually changing we can have no certitude about it by any kind of light, for there can be no certitude when an object is known in some way other than the way in which it is. Neither is there any certitude in knowing a changeable thing as unchangeable. (Ibid., n. 218, 103)[62]

Thus illumination theory also undermines sense certainty.[63] Not only does Henry's theory of illumination preclude knowledge of God and creatures, Scotus believes that Henry's theory of analogy vitiates theological discourse, as Henry denies we can know anything of God's essence (*Ord.* I, d. 3, q. 1, n. 20).

For Henry, illumination furnishes concepts that refer to God, experience furnishes concepts that refer to creatures, and we lack any concepts that pick out both:

> He denies a common concept, univocal to God and creature, and posits two analogous concepts (of which the one, derived from a creature, is attributed to the other, which is of God). (*Ord.* I, d. 22, q. un., nn. 2–3, trans. mine)[64]

The fact that we lack any concept that picks out both God and creatures does not itself render Henry's analogical terms meaningless. The difficulty is that the analogical concepts that characterize God are supposed to tell us what is proper to God's essence without disclosing anything of the essence itself, which Scotus takes to be an impossibility:

> It is naturally possible to have not only a concept in which God is known incidentally, for example, in some attribute, but also

some concept in which he is conceived *per se* and quidditatively. I prove this, because in conceiving 'wise', we conceive a property, according to him [Henry of Ghent], or a quasi-property, which perfects the nature as some further actuality. Hence in order to conceive 'wise', it is necessary to think of some quiddity in which this quasi-property exists. And thus it is necessary to look beyond the ideas of all properties or quasi-properties to some quidditative concept to which we attribute these; and this concept will be a quidditative concept of God, because in no other sort will our quest cease. (*Ord.* I, d. 3, n. 25, *Duns Scotus, Metaphysician,* 109)

For Scotus, to know God's properties is to know something of his essence. Henry is taken to deny this and hence Scotus thinks that Henry's understanding of analogy vitiates theology. Lacking a viable alternative to Henry, Scotus develops the theory that language can univocate God and creatures, but his claim needs to be read in light of his statements that God is wholly simple, and our mediated knowledge of his essence is confused.

*

Scotus believes that God and creatures are characterizable in terms of what pertains to being *qua* being, specifically with reference to its attributes (either coextensive or disjunctive) and perfections. Not everything termed a 'being' exists in the same way. The distance between two objects exists insofar as it is measurable and can be discussed, but this distance ceases to exist as soon as one of the objects is moved and thus distance between objects, while in some sense a being, depends on others for its existence in a way that the objects themselves do not. To capture this and other ways that we use the term 'being', Aristotle posits ten highest genera or categories that comprise its various modes. He offers several different lists, though medieval thinkers viewed that in his *Categories* as authoritative:[65] substance, quantity, quality, relation, place, time, position, state, action, and affection. 'Being' is said of anything in these categories, and is accordingly a transcendental term, as the act of existing transcends any one category of being in the sense that this act is not wholly contained within any one category of being. For his part, Scotus recognized as transcendental those terms that signify: (1) the proper attributes of being; (2) disjunctions comprising attributes of being 'that are opposed to one another such as "possible-or-necessary," "act-or-potency," and suchlike' (*Ord.* I, d. 8, q. 3, *Philosophical Writings*, 3); and (3) the pure perfections. Attributes proper to all beings are unity, truth, and goodness (*Ord.* I, d. 8, q. 3), while each transcendental disjunction exhausts the class of existents. For instance, all beings are either animate or inanimate, possessed of volition or not, and so on. Finally, pure perfections are perfections that are absolutely and without qualification better than anything incompatible with them, meaning that entities not characterizable in terms of pure perfections would be better if they were, even if this meant becoming different types of things (thus it would be better for a plant were it to cease to be a plant and attain wisdom through becoming something else, say an angel or a human) (*De primo princ.* 4.10).[66] Though the pure perfections do not cut across all categories, neither are they subsumed under any genera:

> Just as it is not of the nature of a supreme genus to have many species contained under it, but it is of its nature not to have any genus over and above it … so also whatever is not contained under any genus is transcendental. Hence, not to have any predicate above it except 'being' pertains to the very notion of a transcendental. That it be common to many inferior notions, however, is purely incidental. (*Ord.* I, d. 8, q. 3, *Philosophical Writings*, 3)

Accordingly, terms that signify pure perfections are transcendental.

Transcendental terms signify notions of what pertains to being 'in its indifference to what is infinite and finite [ut est indifferens ad finitum et infinitum]' (ibid., 2), yet joined with the notion of divine infinity they are predicable of God, 'for insofar as they pertain to God they are infinite, whereas insofar as they belong to creatures they are finite' (ibid.). Prescinding from considerations of degree,

transcendental attributes and perfections 'belong to being ... prior
to its division into ten genera' (ibid.). Scotus does not hypostasize
being or view it as a genus above the ten highest genera. Instead, he
believes the ten highest genera are categories of finite being while
God is an infinite being, subsistent and indivisible. Transcendentals
considered apart from degree do not properly, i.e., uniquely, signify
either God or creatures, for all that exists is either finite or infinite.
Thus to acquire proper reference a transcendental must be joined
with the concept of either finitude or infinitude, and in each case
this conjunction produces a new, complex idea. Scotus illustrates
this with reference to our notion of being:

> Every intellect that is certain about one concept, but dubious
> about others has, in addition to the concepts about which it is
> in doubt, another concept of which it is certain ... Now, in this
> life already, a man can be certain in his mind that God is a being
> and still be in doubt whether He is a finite or an infinite being,
> a created or an uncreated being. Consequently, the concept
> of 'being' as affirmed of God is different from the other two
> concepts. (*Ord.* I, d. 3, q. 1, *Philosophical Writings*, 20)

It is important to note that Scotus's apparent admission that 'being'
possesses different though related context-sensitive meanings does
not preclude its core transcendental signification from subsuming
both God and creatures. It is only that this signification does not
uniquely refer to either until joined with the notion of finitude or
infinitude.

Yet while Scotus accepts that terms can signify differently in
different contexts, he denies that they can signify in a prior and
posterior manner:

> [This] seems impossible. For when a name is imposed on a
> secondary thing, it happens to ignore what is simply first since
> what is absolutely posterior can be prior to us, and so it can be
> understood and signified first. If, therefore ... that utterance is
> imposed on something [that is] absolutely first, it is manifest
> that it will [not] signify [that which is absolutely first], through

that secondary [utterance], to which it was first imposed since once it has first signified that [secondary thing], therefore [it will] always [signify it]. For after an utterance has been imposed, it does not change in signifying that to which it was imposed, therefore the order of things does not follow the order in signification of utterances. (*Quaestiones in librum Praedicamentorum*, q. 4, n. 32, trans. Newton)

Scotus places all entities save God on a scale of perfection ordered with respect to degree of being while allowing that God possesses every perfection in the highest possible degree (*Quodl.* 5.9). Thus the divine perfections are absolutely prior. Yet our initial understanding of any perfection emerges from creatures that possess their perfections in a posterior or less eminent manner than God possesses his. Thus terms significative of perfections initially signify creaturely perfections, and Scotus believes that when these terms alter their signification to take in divine perfections it is not the case that the initial significate begins to refer in a prior and posterior manner but rather the terms acquire a new significate that is proper to God. Possessing multiple significates, technically these terms are equivocal.

Scotus's refusal to accept prior and posterior signification developed as a rejection of Modistic semiotics. The *Modistae* distinguish equivocal terms from analogical terms on the grounds that only the former retain their multiple related significates outside of linguistic context. Yet in sentential context, the two types of terms function in the same way. In the case of analogical terms, the *Modistae* posited that in the original act of imposition the name-giver stipulated a set of instructions that allow for the decoding of these terms in sentential context, but Scotus believes that this speculation as regards the original act of imposition is unfounded. Thus he rejects the existence of analogical terms that signify different though related ideas and insists that these terms are equivocal.[67] This is not to say that he rejects the idea that equivocal terms can signify various complex concepts that are related through a core univocal idea—we have seen him embrace this notion in his discussion of the related senses of 'being.' What he denies is that one and the same idea can refer primarily to God and secondarily to creatures. In cases of primary and secondary reference, Scotus believes that we have different though related ideas.

Terms said of God and creatures have multiple significates owing to their origin in experience, which is of creatures not God. Yet the transcendental ideas that refer to God are related to the transcendental ideas that refer to creatures, the only difference between the two is that the ideas referred to God are joined with the notion of infinitude while those referred to creatures are joined with the notion of finitude; for the conjunction with infinitude does not alter the content of the transcendental idea that prescinds from any consideration of degree.[68] Yet though the conjunction with infinitude does not alter the content of a transcendental idea, this conjunction does create a new idea that refers properly to God. What does this idea tell us of God's essence?

When a transcendental concept is joined with the notion of infinitude, we 'obtain a concept which is proper to God in the sense that it is characteristic of no other being' (*Quodl.* 14.13). Note this concept is proper in the sense that it refers uniquely to God. Infinitude thus serves as a marker, rendering the complex concept proper to God without altering its content. Yet how accurate a representation of God's essence is the initial transcendental concept? Its content seems fairly straightforward: some trait experienced in creation abstracting from considerations pertaining to degree. What makes this trait unique to God is its conjunction with infinitude. So to determine what transcendental concepts tell us of God's essence we should look to Scotus's discussions of infinitude, which indicate that though infinitude has no bearing on meaning at the conceptual level, Scotus nonetheless acknowledges the difference between creator and creation at the ontological level. Importing these considerations into Scotus's theory of transcendental signification may clarify our picture of what it does and does not tell us of God's essence.

Owing to his infinitude, God 'exceeds any finite being whatsoever not in some limited degree but in a measure beyond what is either defined or can be defined' (*Quodl.* 5.9). Moreover, owing to his infinitude God is unique; there cannot be more than one infinite being (*De primo princ.* 4.87–93). Hence, owing to his infinitude God differs in kind from every other being in existence. Scotus likens God's infinitude to a quantitatively infinite in act. Like the quantitatively infinite in act (conceived as an actually existent infinite quantity), what is infinite in being cannot be exceeded in being by any other entity. Thus it possesses every perfection of being and is infinite 'in perfection or power' (*Quodl.* 5.8). Moreover, 'an infinite being ... is perfect in such a way that neither it nor any of its parts is missing anything' (ibid., n. 7). That is, no part lacks any other, for each infinite part must equal the infinite whole (*De primo princ.* 4.76).

Concepts referred to God characterize an entity unlike any we are ever likely to encounter in this life. Our knowledge of God is mediated (*Quodl.* 14.74) and dimly represents his essence (ibid., n. 89). Nonetheless, transcendental signification provides accurate knowledge of God (*Ord.* I, d. 3, pars. 1, q. 2, n. 40). We have seen that Scotus likens transcendentals referred to God as confused along the lines that the concept of man merely as some type of animal is confused (*Quodl.* 14.13). In a report (*reportatio*) taken from his lectures, Scotus clarifies both what positive knowledge these concepts provide as well as why they are confused. Here Scotus locates our confused knowledge of God on a scale comprising four levels of epistemic access to an entity, with knowledge of God at the penultimate level, the highest level reserved for the conception of an entity in terms of its genus and specific difference (*Ord.* I, d. 22, q. un., Appendix A). The same discussion makes it clear that our finite minds cannot grasp infinite being.[69] This suggests that our knowledge of God is limited to the penultimate level (where one grasps an entity's genus but not the specific difference that contracts that genus) because we cannot grasp his infinitude, which here functions along the lines of a specific difference. This again points to the regulative function infinitude serves in Scotus's understanding of theological discourse. The conjunction with infinitude does not provide new knowledge so much as regulate the transfer of knowledge from creation to creator in a manner comparable to Aquinas's ways of eminence, causality and remotion. The conjunction with infinitude warns against supposing that concepts of isolated perfections and attributes provide anything save abstract notions of the divine essence, whose infinitude is attended with absolute simplicity. Concepts refer to God and creatures without any alteration whatsoever but can never accurately represent how the attributes and perfections they grasp inhere in God's essence.

Scotus claims we possess terms univocal to God and creatures, but insists that concepts referred to God be joined with the notion of infinitude. This stipulation seems intended to account for God's unity in diversity and the limitations this places on our knowledge of his essence. Thus Scotus follows Aquinas in adapting the signification of theological discourse to account for the radical difference between creator and creation; and Scotus's talk of univocity does not indicate a brash break with tradition.

*

Chapter 2 examines Aquinas's understanding of apodictic or scientific knowledge (*scientia*). This serves two purposes. First, it clarifies Aquinas's understanding of scientific demonstration (and thus knowledge in general), which enables me to argue in Chapter 3 that Aquinas's Five Ways are scientific demonstrations. Recalling Aquinas's stipulation that theological discourse is analogical, if the Five Ways are demonstrations, Aquinas's understanding of the information provided by demonstration will help us understand what Aquinas believes we can know of God and this, in turn, will shed further light on Aquinas's understanding of analogy of attribution. Second, the discussion in Chapter 2 of Aquinas's views about *scientia* allows me to contrast Aquinas and Scotus on this point in Chapter 4, thus substantiating the claim made above that Scotus is more circumspect than Aquinas on this point, and also clarifying what Scotus believes we can know of God inasmuch as his views on our knowledge of God are related to his conception of knowledge in general. Chapters 5 and 6 consider why Scotus locates our knowledge of God at the penultimate level of the aforementioned fourfold scale comprising our levels of epistemic access to an entity and what this move tells us about his understanding of univocity in theological discourse. Finally, Chapter 7 revisits the argument that Scotus's rejection of analogy and development of univocity does not put him at odds with Aquinas as concerns the boundaries of natural theology.

Chapter 2

Aquinas and *Scientia*

'*Scientia*' is the Latin translation of the Greek 'ἐπιστήμη.' Both terms may be translated as 'knowledge.' The technical sense of this term whereby it connotes scientific knowledge developed in the works of philosophers such as Parmenides, Heraclitus, and Plato, who discuss whether we can attain certainty about what is apparently an ever-changing world. Yet it is Aristotle's later conception of scientific knowledge that most influenced scholastic thought.

Aristotle's most thorough treatment of *scientia* is given in his *Posterior Analytics* (*An.Post*). Studying this work in conjunction with Aquinas's commentary will help clarify the latter's understanding of scientific knowledge. At the beginning of the *Posterior Analytics* Aristotle raises the topic of *scientia* by way of an aporia (*An.Post* I 1). A man is asked whether he knows that everything that is a pair is even-numbered. When he replies that he does, the questioner produces a pair that the man did not know to exist and consequently could not have known to be even-numbered.[1] This aporia points immediately to one of the main concerns of the *Posterior Analytics*, the explanation of our ability to discern the essential predicates that distinguish various natural kinds.

It would be inappropriate for Aristotle's respondent to concede that while all of the pairs with which he is familiar are even-numbered sets he does not know with respect to every pair that this is so (*An.Post* I 1, 71ᵃ33–34). Rather, he somehow (πως) knew that the newly introduced pair would be even-numbered, but did not know that this particular pair existed (*An.Post* I 1, 71ᵇ5–7). But, how do we know with certainty that some predicate *F* is distributed with respect to an entire class though we have not encountered each and every member of this class; put another way, what is the sense of Aristotle's '*πως*'?

Aristotle's discussion of *scientia* is his answer to this question. On Aquinas's interpretation, *scientia* is apodictic because it is of what belongs to a thing owing to its essence or nature (In PA I.4 & II.1, 8, 9), but this does not mean that scientific ascriptions always signify the essence of a thing. In some cases scientific propositions provide 'some hold' on a thing through effects necessarily connected (and thus proper) to its nature rather than the nature itself (*An.Post* II 8, 93ª29). Aristotle supplies the example of thunder, which may be described either as 'sound in a cloud' or 'extinction of fire in a cloud' (*An.Post* II 8, 93ᵇ8). Both ascriptions always pertain to thunder but only the latter defines the phenomenon in terms of essential predicates (*An.Post* II 8, 93ª14–ᵇ21).[2] Essential predicates supply what are called 'real' definitions, while definitions that rely on proper effects are termed 'nominal.'

For Aquinas, paradigmatic *scientia* is the result of syllogistic reasoning (In PA I.10.8 & I.13, n. 3 = *An.Post* I 4, 73ᵇ16–17 & I 6, 74ᵇ6–12). Syllogisms productive of *scientia* use either real or nominal definitions as their middle, and thus the conclusion tells us what belongs to the subject through itself or *per se*. *Per se* belonging lies at the heart of *scientia*.

Per Se Belonging

'*Per se*' is the Latin translation of Aristotle's '*καθ᾽ αὑτό.*' Aquinas's discussion of *per se* belonging focuses primarily on four applications of the phrase '*per se*' and relates the three of these that he believes are relevant to *scientia* to Aristotle's explanation of causality in terms of material, formal, efficient, and final causes. Aristotle defines these causes (in this order) as follows:

We call a cause (1) that from which (as immanent material) a thing comes into being, e.g., the bronze of the statue ... (2) The form or pattern, i.e., the formula of the essence, and the classes which include this ... and the parts of the formula. (3)

> That from which the change or the freedom from change first
> begins, e.g., the man who has deliberated is a cause and the
> father a cause of the child ... (4) The end, i.e., that for the
> sake of which a thing is, e.g., health is the cause of walking.
> (*Met* V 2, 1013ª24–36)

Aquinas views this list as authoritative though material causality
is not clearly present in the list of the four causes that Aristotle
furnishes in his *Posterior Analytics*.[3]

> There are four types of explanation (one, what it is to be a thing;
> one, that if certain things hold it is necessary that this does;
> another, what initiated the change; and the fourth, the aim).
> (*An.Post* II 11, 94ª21–23)

Nonetheless, Aquinas identifies the second cause, 'that if certain
things hold it is necessary that this does,' with Aristotle's material
cause (In PA II.9.2 = *An.Post* II 11, 94ª20–95ª9).

Aquinas draws a connection between Aristotle's four causes and
the notion of *per se* belonging with the claim that the first, second,
and fourth applications of the phrase '*per se*' (those Aquinas views
as relevant to *scientia*) pick out different ways that entities act as
causes with respect to themselves.[4] In the first instance, an entity
is viewed as a cause with respect to itself as concerns the attributes
signified through its real definition, in this way rationality and
animality belong *per se* to human beings. Aquinas believes that
this inherence obtains through formal causality. The second type
of *per se* belonging occurs when a subject (acting as a material
cause) is responsible for its proper or *per se* accidents, which are
attributes definable only in terms of their subject, as the definition
of 'aquilinity' must incorporate 'nose' since aquilinity is nothing
other than a property of noses (though noses are not necessarily
aquiline) (In PA I.10.4 = *An.Post* I 4, 73ª37–ᵇ4). The fourth instance
of *per se* belonging takes in any way that a subject can act as a cause
with respect to itself. Thus every instance of the first and second
type of *per se* belonging is an instance of the fourth (though it is
unclear whether Aquinas accepts the converse). This type of *per*

se belonging comprises all four Aristotelian causes (In PA I.10.7). Aquinas uses Aristotle's example of something dying because it is killed to illustrate this causality (In PA I.10.7 = *An.Post* I.4, 73^b10–15).

Here is Aristotle's account of the relevant types of *per se* belonging, the Latin translation, and Aquinas's commentary. The English is taken from the Latin:[5]

(1) *An.Post* I 4, 73^a34–35 = In PA I.10

- Καθ᾽ αὑτὰ δ᾽ ὅσα ὑπάρχει ἐν τῷ τί ἐστιν, οἷον τριγώνῳ γραμμὴ.
- *Per se autem sunt quecunque sunt in eo quod quid est, ut triangulo inest linea.*
- *Per se* attributes are such as belong to their subject as elements in its essential nature, as line is in a triangle.

Aquinas's Commentary (In PA I.10.3)

- *Primus modus eius quod est per se est, quando praedicatur de aliquo definitio vel aliquid in definitione positum.*
- The first mode of that which is *per se* is when the definition itself or something expressed in the definition is predicated of the thing defined.

(2) *An.Post* I 4, 73^a37–39 = In PA I.10

- Καθ᾽ αὑτὰ δ᾽ ὅσα ὑπάρχει ἐν … αὑτοῖς αὑτὰ ἐν τῷ λόγῳ ἐνυπάρχουσι τῷ τί ἐστι δηλοῦντι.
- *Per se [sunt] … quibuscunque eorum que insunt subiectis, ipsa in ratione insunt quid est demonstranti, ut rectum inest linee et circulare.*
- *Per se* [properties] are … any of those that belong to subjects,[6] which subjects themselves are in the formula demonstrating the definition [of these properties], as straight and curved belong to line *per se* [trans. mine].

Aquinas's Commentary (In PA I.10.4)

- *Secundus modus dicendi per se est quando subiectum ponitur in diffinitione predicati quod est proprium accidens eius.*

- It is the second mode of saying *per se*, when the subject is mentioned in the definition of a predicate which is a proper accident of the subject.

(4) *An.Post* I4, 73ᵇ10–16

- Ἔτι δ᾽ ἄλλον τρόπον τὸ μὲν δι᾽ αὑτὸ ὑπάρχον ἑκάστῳ καθ᾽ αὑτο, τὸ δὲ μὴ δι᾽ αὑτὸ συμβεβηκός, οἷον ... εἴ τι σφαττόμενον ἀπέθανε, καὶ κατὰ τὴν σφαγήν, ὅτι διὰ τὸ σφάττεσθαι, ἀλλ᾽ οὐ συνέβη σφαττόμενον ἀποθανεῖν.
- *Item alio modo quod quidem propter ipsum inest unicuique per se, quod vero non propter ipsum accidens est ... Ut si aliquod inter-fectum interiit, secundum interfectionem, quoniam propter id quod interfectum est, set non quod accidat interfectum interire.*
- Again, in another way, what is in each and every thing [it is in] on account of itself is *per se*, but what is not in something on account of itself is an accident ... For example, if something dies, having been slaughtered, because of the slaughter (since [its death] is on account of its having been slaughtered, but it is not the case that being slaughtered it [just] happens to die) [trans. mine].

Aquinas's commentary (In PA I.10.7)

- *Haec praepositio per designat habitudinem causae efficientis vel cuiuscunque alterius. Et ideo dicit quod quidquid inest unicuique propter seipsum, per se dicitur de eo; quod vero non propter seipsum inest alicui, per accidens dicitur.*
- [In the fourth mode] the preposition '*per*' designates a relationship of efficient cause or of any other. Consequently he says that 'whatever is attributed to a thing because of itself, is said of it *per se*, but whatever is not so attributed is said *per accidens*.'

An.Post I 4, 73ᵇ16–18

In chapter 4 of the *Posterior Analytics*, Aristotle presents the types of *per se* belonging that are relevant to scientific knowledge. His discussion is terse and ambiguous, and Aquinas's interpretation is at odds with modern commentators, likely owing to several apparent errors in the transmission from the Greek to Latin.[7] The passage reads:

Τὰ ἄρα λεγόμενα ἐπι τῶν ἁπλῶς ἐπιστητῶν καθ' αὐτὰ—οὕτως ὡς ἐνυπάρχειν τοῖς κατηγορουμένοις ἢ ἐνυπάρχεσθαι—δι' αὐτά τέ ἐστι καὶ ἐξ ἀνάγκης (*An.Post* 73ᵇ16–18).

Therefore, in the case of what is absolutely scientifically knowable, the things called '*per se*'—in the following manner, viz., as belonging to the predicates or as belonged to—are [*per se*] on account of themselves and by necessity [trans. mine].

Que ergo dicuntur in simpliciter scibilibus per se sic sunt, sicut inesse predicantibus aut inesse propter ipsa. Que sunt necessitate.

Therefore, in the case of what is absolutely scientifically knowable, the things called '*per se*' are [*per se*] in this way,[8] they belong to predicates or are in them on account of themselves. These things are by necessity [trans. mine].

The first way the Latin and Greek differ arises from an ambiguity inherent in 'κατηγορουμένοις.' This term is a passive participle of 'κατηγορεῖν,' meaning 'to speak against' or 'accuse,' which in the context of Aristotelian logic is translated 'to predicate.' Thus 'κατηγορουμένοις' (literally 'the things accused') can refer either to the subjects of predication, which are accused of possessing certain predicates, or to the predicates that are accused of these subjects.[9] Modern translations reflect this ambiguity, with Ross and Tredennick choosing 'subjects,'[10] while Barnes's revised Oxford translation has 'predicates.'[11] Choosing 'subjects' makes the two instances of *per se* belonging that are relevant to *scientia* instances where things belong to or are belonged to by a subject. Ross and Tredennick identify the instances thus formulated with the first and second types of *per se* belonging, respectively, thus what belongs to a subject is its definition and what is belonged to by a subject are its proper accidents.[12] Tredennick goes so far as to say that the third and fourth types of *per se* belonging are irrelevant and perhaps added by another hand.[13]

If however 'κατηγορουμένοις' means 'predicates,' and we understand by 'predicate' the predicate term in a scientific proposition, then what (1) belongs to or (2) is belonged to by the predicate is the subject term, on the grounds that scientific propositions are definitions (*An.Post* II 3, 90ᵇ25; & II 10) whose terms are coextensive (*An. Post* II 13, 96ᵃ32–34) and thus contain and are contained by one another. Again this can be read as a description of the first and second types of *per se* belonging. When the subject term belongs to the predicate term this would be an assertion of the second type of *per se* belonging, where the subject term signifies a proper accident and the ontological subject to which it belongs is named in its definition, as the definition of 'aquilinity' mentions noses. Conversely, when the subject term is belonged to by the predicate term it can be said to possess the predicate in the manner that an entity possesses its definition and we would have an instance of the first type of *per se* belonging.

For his part, Aquinas takes 'κατηγορουμένοις' ('*predicantibus*' in the Latin) to refer to proper accidents which are predicated of ontological subjects (and thus may be termed 'predicates'); and he believes that this passage describes the second and fourth types of *per se* belonging, respectively. Here again is the translation from the Latin:

> Therefore, in the case of what is absolutely scientifically knowable, the things called '*per se*' are [*per se*] in this way, they belong to predicates or are in them on account of themselves. These things are by necessity [trans. mine].

The first reference to *per se* belonging has it that things termed '*per se*' belong to predicates. What belongs to a predicate (understood as a proper accident) is its ontological subject, thus Aquinas identifies this as a formulation of the second type of *per se* belonging, which describes how subjects belong to their proper accidents, viz., in their definitions (In PA I.10.8 = *An.Post* I 4, 73ᵇ16–17). The second sense given is one where things 'belong on account of themselves [*inesse propter ipsa*],' which Aquinas identifies with the fourth type of *per se* belonging, motivated perhaps by the Latin description of the fourth type of *per se* belonging as obtaining when something belongs to a subject 'on account of itself [*propter ipsum*]' (*An.Post* I 4, 73ᵇ16). In addition, Aquinas believes this passage discusses the conclusions of scientific demonstrations. A conclusion is a single statement, yet Aristotle speaks of two types of *per se* belonging. Aquinas's belief that Aristotle's discussion is of the second and fourth types of *per se* belonging enables him to reconcile this apparent disparity, for the fourth type of *per se* belonging takes in all others (In PA I.10.7), hence an assertion of the second is likewise an assertion of the fourth.

The ambiguity of '*κατηγορουμένοις*' aside, there is a key variance between the Latin and Greek texts, for the Latin misconstrues Aristotle's '*τε ... και*' ('both ... and') construction:

Τὰ ἄρα λεγόμενα ἐπὶ τῶν ἁπλῶς ἐπιστητῶν καθ᾽ αὑτὰ—οὕτως ὡς ἐνυπάρχειν τοῖς κατηγορουμένοις ἢ ἐνυπάρχεσθαι—δι᾽ αὑτά τέ ἐστι καὶ ἐξ ἀνάγκης. (*An.Post* 73ᵇ16–18)

Therefore, in the case of what is absolutely scientifically knowable, the things called '*per se*'—in the following manner, viz., as belonging to the predicates or as belonged to—are [*per se*] on account of themselves and by necessity [trans. mine].

Que ergo dicuntur in simpliciter scibilibus per se sic sunt, sicut inesse predicantibus aut inesse propter ipsa. Que sunt necessitate.

Therefore, in the case of what is absolutely scientifically knowable, the things called '*per se*' are [*per se*] in this way, as they belong to predicates or are in them on account of themselves. These things are by necessity [trans. mine].

'*τε*' alone means 'and' or 'but.' However, as in this passage, '*τε*' is more commonly used as a correlative in combination with '*και*' ('and' or 'even') to unite similar and opposite complements. Functioning correlatively '*τε*' and '*και*' unites its complements and can be translated with 'both … and', or simply 'and.' Respectively, 'τε' and 'καί' follow and precede the terms that they unite. In addition, 'τε' is postpositive, meaning that it usually comes right after the first word in its sentence or clause.

In our passage, 'τε' belongs with 'δι᾽ αὐτά (on account of themselves).' This phrase 'on account of themselves' complements what follows 'καί', viz., 'ἐξ ἀνάγκης (by necessity).' Thus, the presence of Arisotle's 'τε … καί' construction shows that 'on account of themselves' complements 'by necessity,' and not 'ἐνυπάρχεσθαι (to be belonged to).' Moreover, since 'τε' is postpositive, the phrase that it joins with forms a new clause; specifically, it picks up the main clause that is interrupted by Aristotle's parenthetical description of the two applications of the phrase '*per se*' that are relevant to *scientia*. The Leonine edition does not reflect Aristotle's construction. Translating 'δι᾽ αὐτά' with '*propter ipsa* (on account of themselves),' and the middle-passive infinitive 'ἐνυπάρχεσθαι (to be belonged to)' with the active infinitive '*inesse* (to belong),' the Latin links '*inesse*' with '*propter ipsa.*' As a consequence, Aristotle's parenthetical description is expanded at the expense of his main clause: the second use of '*per se*' becomes one where things are not simply 'belonged to' but rather one where they 'are in [subjects] on account of themselves,' and the phrase 'on account of themselves' no longer modifies the subject of the main clause, viz., whatever a demonstrator terms '*per se*,' but rather only Aristotle's description of the second use of *per se* belonging relevant to *scientia*.

In addition, the Latin introduces an instance of the verb 'to be' not present in the Greek. Aristotle's sentence is governed by the verb 'ἐστι.' Greek often uses this singular form of the verb 'to be' with a plural subject, accordingly the Latin translates it with '*sunt* (they are).' Yet, the Latin has '*sunt*' twice. This is so not only in the Leonine, but in the critical reconstruction of James's edition as well, which reads:

> *Que ergo dicuntur in simpliciter scibilibus per se sic <u>sunt</u>, sicut inesse predicantibus aut inesse propter ipsaque <u>sunt</u> et ex necessitate.*

Were we to remove the first '*sunt*,' this passage would reflect the meaning of the Greek, capturing as it does Aristotle's '*τε* ... *και*' construction by means of the Latin conjunctive, enclitic particle '*-que*' along with '*et.*' Yet, in medieval Latin, '*que*' is also used in place of '*quae* (these things),' the neuter plural of the relative pronoun '*qui.*' Following Aquinas's commentary, the Leonine edition draws on this second use of '*que*' for its translation. Now, Minio-Paluello's apparatus does not give us any reason to take '*que*' as a relative pronoun. It does, however, note that '*et*' is missing in several manuscripts. This may provide a clue as to why Aquinas's text misconstrues the Greek. The double presence of '*sunt*' in James's translation presents Aristotle's one sentence as if it were two. Moreover, in the manuscripts where '*et*' is missing, that omission leaves '*que*' without a correlative. Faced with such a manuscript, the decision to look on James's '*que*' as a relative pronoun serving as the subject of a new sentence rather than a correlative conjunction would make sense. As for the double '*sunt,*' though Ross's apparatus does not indicate a double '*ἐστι,*' Minio-Paluello's shows no indication of a manuscript of James's translation that has but one '*sunt,*' so it is difficult to determine the cause of this difference, though we may note in passing that neither John's nor Moerbeke's *recensiones* have the extra '*sunt.*' Let us now turn to Aquinas's commentary on this passage, divided below into three sections.

Aquinas's Commentary (In PA I.10.8)

(1) [Aristotle] shows how the demonstrator uses the aforesaid modes (73^{b}16). Since science bears on conclusions, and understanding [*intellectus*] ... on principles, the scientifically knowable are, properly speaking, the conclusions of a demonstration wherein proper attributes are predicated of their appropriate subjects.

The 'aforementioned modes' are the first, second, and fourth types of *per se* belonging, which constitute various ways that subjects serve as the ground of their essential predicates. 'Properly speaking' *scientia* is of a demonstration's conclusion. This stipulation emerges from Aquinas's recognition of a distinction between '*scientia*' and '*intellectus* (intellection)' (sometimes Aquinas uses '*cognitio* (cognition)' in place of '*intellectus*,' e.g., In PA I.7.1). *Scientia* is the product of a demonstration, while *intellectus* is a grasp of the immediate principles of demonstration. An immediate principle of demonstration is a proposition true by definition, for instance that a whole is greater than its parts (In PA I.7.8). *Intellectus* differs from *scientia* because *scientia* requires a demonstration through a middle that is a definition, while *intellectus* is the immediate recognition of the necessity of a proposition. Yet not all *scientia* is the product of demonstration from immediate first principles. For conclusions that are known scientifically can serve as the premises of scientific demonstrations, provided these conclusions are ultimately derived from immediate first principles (In PA I.4.14).

> (2) Now the appropriate subjects are not only placed in the definition of attributes, but they are also their causes. Hence the conclusions of demonstrations involve two modes of predicating *per se*, namely, the second and the fourth. And this is what he means when he says that predications 'in the case of what is absolutely scientifically knowable,' i.e., in the conclusions of demonstrations, are *per se* 'as they belong to the predicates [*sicut inesse praedicantibus*],' i.e., in the way that subjects are contained in the definition of accidents which are predicated of the former; or 'are in them on account of themselves [*inesse propter ipsa*],' i.e., in the way that predicates are in a subject by reason of the subject itself, which is the cause of the predicate.[14]

Aquinas grounds this use of the second and fourth types of *per se* belonging in Aristotle's text ('*et hoc est quod dicit*'). The conclusion of a scientific demonstration formulates two types of *per se* belonging. Ascriptions are *per se* as they (1) 'belong to the predicates' or (2) 'are in them on account of themselves.' Aquinas interprets 'predicates' to mean 'proper accidents' (which are predicated of their ontological subjects), and we have seen how he construes

Aristotle's discussion in terms of the second and fourth types of *per se* belonging, respectively. Given Aquinas's understanding of the broad role played by the fourth type of *per se* belonging, allotting this type of *per se* belonging a place in the conclusions of scientific demonstrations seems to make room for assertions of the first type as well. Yet Aquinas will later specify that the conclusion of a scientific demonstration must be an assertion of the second type of *per se* belonging (In PA I.13 = *An.Post* I 6, 74^{b}6–12).

> (3) Then he shows that such scientifically knowable things are necessary, because it is impossible for a proper accident not to be predicated of its subject. But this can occur in two ways: sometimes it is absolute, as when a single accident is convertible with its subject, as 'having three angles equal to two right angles' is convertible with triangle, and 'risible' with man. At other times, two opposites stated disjunctively are of necessity in the subject, 'as "straight or oblique" in line.'

Aquinas concludes by elaborating on Aristotle's distinction between two types of proper accidents. One type is convertible with the subject to which it belongs. Yet though convertible or counter-predicable with their subjects,[15] these proper accidents do not enter into the formulae that define their subjects.[16] For instance, all humans are thought to be risible yet risibility does not figure into the definition of 'human being.' The second type of proper accidents are groupings of mutually exclusive properties that are coextensive with certain types of things, as odd and even together are coextensive with number.[17] In either case the ascription of *per se* belonging is necessary.[18]

Scientia

Aristotle gives '$\dot{\epsilon}\pi\iota\sigma\tau\dot{\eta}\mu\eta$ (*scientia*)' a technical meaning when he distinguishes between accidental (*secundum accidens*) and unqualified (*simpliciter*) knowing, and identifes *scientia* proper with the latter (*An.Post* I 2, 71ᵇ9–16 = In PA I.4.4). We possess *scientia*, or judge that we know a thing unqualifiedly, 'when we also judge that we know the cause on account of which the thing is; and, since it is the cause of the thing, we know as well that it is not possible that it be otherwise than it is' (*An.Post* I 2, 71ᵇ9–12 = In PA I.4.4, 5, trans. mine).[19]

Aquinas sees three elements at work in this definition of '*scientia*' (In PA I.4.5 = *An.Post* I 2, 71ᵇ10–11). *Scientia* is knowledge of: (1) the cause of what is known (*causa rei*), (2) the application of the cause to its effect (*applicatio causae ad effectum*), and (3) the fact that what is known could not be otherwise (*non possit aliter se habere*) and is accordingly necessary.

(1) What is known scientifically can be given as the conclusion of a scientific demonstration (In PA I.10.8 = *An.Post* I 4, 73ᵇ16–17). The logical and ontological cause of the conclusion of such a demonstration is the middle term (In PA II.1.8 = *An. Post.* II 2, 90ᵃ5–11),[20] which is either the nominal or the real definition of the subject (*An. Post* II 8–10). *Scientia*, then, entails knowledge of this middle or cause, sometimes referred to as a principle of demonstration (In PA I.3.1 & I.4.5). (2) But merely to possess knowledge of these principles is insufficient. They are also efficient causes of knowledge and one must grasp their causality. Just as in nature a potential efficient cause may or may not produce a certain effect, so too in demonstrative matters one may know certain principles but fail to understand how they are employed in the demonstration of some conclusion (In PA I.3.1 = *An.Post* I 1, 24–28). Someone in this position possesses a virtual (*virtute*) knowledge of the conclusion. This is to be contrasted with the unqualified knowledge of one who knows scientifically and thus possesses the demonstration and with it actual (*in actu*) knowledge. (3) Finally, as *scientia* is certain, it cannot be of what is capable of being otherwise.

Consequently,

Because ... *scientia* is perfect knowledge, he [Aristotle] says 'when we also judge that we know the cause'; but because it is the actual knowledge through which we know scientifically, he adds 'and, since it is the cause of the thing.' Finally, because it is certain knowledge, he adds, 'it is not possible that it be otherwise than it is.' (In PA I.4.5 = *An.Post* I 271^{b}10–11)[21]

In PA I.13.3 = *An.Post* I 6, 74^{b}6-12: The Scientific Syllogism

Scientia is knowledge of what is necessarily true of a subject, in the sense that scientific ascriptions cannot cease to be true. This is why scientific knowledge is of universals rather than ephemeral particulars, informing us about individuals only to the extent that they are members of some natural kind.[22] The reason that *scientia* cannot be otherwise is that it is built on *per se* predication. We have seen that Aquinas believes three types of *per se* predication are relevant to scientific knowledge, and each type plays a particular role in Aquinas's paradigmatic scientific syllogism.

The major premise of the paradigm (AAA-1) scientific syllogism predicates the fourth type of *per se* belonging, in which the attribute signified by the major term is said to belong *per se* to the subject of the demonstration, which is signified by the middle term. The minor premise predicates the first type of *per se* belonging; the definition signified by the middle term is said to belong *per se* to the subject of the demonstration, itself signified by the minor term. For its part, the conclusion is an assertion of the second type of *per se* belonging,[23] in which the attribute signified by the major term is said to belong *per se* to the subject signified by the minor term. For example: 'The rational animal is risible; man is the rational animal; therefore, man is risible.'

We are now in a better position to understand what the scientific knower knows and why he or she knows it. What is known is that an attribute belongs necessarily to a subject. The cause of this belonging is the subject itself, and that this subject is the cause is demonstrated through a syllogism showing that the attribute belongs to the subject by definition, whether nominal or real.

Types of Scientific Demonstration

Aquinas believes that the first book of the *Posterior Analytics* was written to explain the demonstrative syllogism and the second to discuss its parts, viz., the middle term and first principles (In PA II.1.1). First principles, described variously as 'axioms (ἀξιώματα),' 'common opinions (κοιναὶ δόξαι),' or 'common things (τὰ κοινά),'[24] are the indemonstrable principles upon which demonstration depends:

> It is necessary for demonstrative scientific knowledge ... to depend on things which are true and primitive and immediate and more familiar than and prior to and explanatory of the conclusion ... For there will be deduction even without these conditions, but there will not be demonstration; for it will not produce scientific knowledge. (*An.Post* I 2, 71ᵇ19–25)

Axioms are of two types: the rules governing inference,[25] and principles unique to one science. An example of the former is the principle of non-contradiction. The latter type of axiom, on the other hand, comprises assumptions about the existence of the science's subject matter along with definitions of the subject matter's manifestations.[26] For example, geometry assumes the existence of magnitude along with the definitions of certain magnitudes such as triangles. These definitions, however, make no claims about the existence of the definiendum. We may term such definitions 'axiomatic definitions,' to indicate their role as indemonstrable first principles of demonstration. The middle terms of demonstrations, for their part, are used to link subject and predicate and thereby to aid us in discovering what belongs *per se* to the subject (In PA II.1.1 = *An.Post* II 1, 89ᵃ21–90ᵇ35). Accordingly, Aquinas follows Aristotle and begins his commentary on the second book of the *Posterior Analytics* by discussing just which questions middle terms are employed to answer.

There are four such questions, corresponding to four types of things that admit of being known with scientific certainty. The questions are: '*Quia* (Is it a fact that __?)'; '*Propter quid* (Why/What is the cause or reason for __?)'; '*Si est* (If/Whether it is, e.g., Does __ exist?)'; and '*Quid est* (What is __?)'.[27] These questions are first divided into simple and complex. The simple questions ('*Si est*' and '*Quid est*') are answered with a noun and a verb, without an appositive, while the complex ones ('*Quia*' and '*Propter quid*') set some third term with the other two:

> As is stated in *On Interpretation* II, the proposition is formed in two ways: in one way from a noun and a verb without any appositive, as when it is stated that *a man is*; in another way when some third item is set adjacent, as when it is stated that *a man is white*. Therefore the questions we form can be reduced either to the first type of proposition so that we get, as it were, a simple question; or to the second type, and then the question will be, as it were, complex or *put in number*, because, namely, the question concerns the putting together of two items. (In PA II.1.3)

Thus, the answer to a *quia* question takes the form of, 'It is a fact that (___) is (_____),' whereas the answer to a *si est* question is either '(___) exists' or '(___) does not exist.' Aquinas then distinguishes between types of simple and complex questions by noting that *quia* and *si est* questions ask whether something is while *propter quid* and *quid est* questions ask what something is, producing the following divisions:

Questions Pertaining to *Scientia*

	(1) Simple	(2) Complex
(A) Is it?	If/Whether it is, e.g., Does ___ exist (*si est*)?	Is it a fact that ___ is ___ (*quia*)?
(B) What is it?	What is ___ (*quid est*)?	Why/What is the cause or reason that ___ is ___ (*propter quid*)?

These divisions emerge from the role of the middle term in scientific demonstration. Questions in group (A) ask nothing 'else than whether or not a middle term is to be found of that which we ask' (In PA II.1.6). Here the middle term signifies some phenomenon that reveals that something is the case. For example, were one to ask whether it is the case that there is now an eclipse of the moon (defined as the interposition of the earth between the sun and the moon), the following demonstration would supply the answer by drawing on a certain phenomenon, viz., that the moon is currently unable to produce a shadow:

> The moon cannot now produce the shadow of an object placed between it and us.
> <u>Whenever the moon is thus unable to produce a shadow, the moon is eclipsed.</u>
> Therefore, the moon is now eclipsed.

Knowing *that* (*quia*) something is the case, one can then investigate *why* (*propter quid*) it is the case. These latter demonstrations account for an effect through a middle that offers insight into the nature of the cause of the effect (In PA II.1.8). For instance:

> An eclipse is the interposition of the earth between sun and moon.
> <u>Such an interposition is presently affecting the moon.</u>
> Therefore, there is now an eclipse.

This syllogism is constructed by one who knows that the moon receives light from the sun and that this received light allows the moon to cast shadows. An eclipse of the moon is definable as an event resulting from the interposition of the earth between the sun and the moon that renders the moon unable to receive the light of the sun. With this understanding of the nature of an eclipse, one can explain the occurrence of an eclipse in terms of what it is to be an eclipse, thus the answer to the question *why* is the same as the answer to the question *what* (In PA II.1.8).

Aristotle also provides an example having to do with concordance (συμφωνία), to show that the question *why* is equivalent to the question *what*:

> What is concordance? An arithmetical ratio between high and low. Why does the high concord with the low? Because an arith-

metical ratio holds between the high and the low. (*An.Post* II 2, 90ª19–21)[28]

Then, still using the example of concordance, Aristotle shows how questions in group (A) lead naturally to questions in group (B), that is, how when we have determined *that* or *whether* something is the case we next inquire *why* it is the case: 'Can the high and the low concord?—Is there an arithmetical ratio between them? Assuming that there is, what then is the ratio?' (ibid., 21–23). The *that* (*quia*) question asks if it is the case that there is a numerical ratio (concordance) between the high and low notes. This is followed with the *why* (*propter quid*) question that asks why these notes concord, which is to ask what is the ratio between them (for *what* and *why* questions are equivalent). The *quia* question is answered with the following demonstration:

Notes possessing a numerical ratio are concordant.
<u>These high and low notes possess a numerical ratio.</u>
Therefore, these high and low notes are concordant.

But Aquinas believes that this example requires special consideration, remarking that this *quia* demonstration uses a proper attribute's definition as its middle (In PA II.1.9). With this comment, Aquinas proceeds to show why this is not an entirely accurate appraisal of the syllogism.

Yet before we examine his discussion, let us consider why Aquinas feels compelled to dwell on this point. At least some of his motivation lies in his understanding of the structure of the scientific syllogism:

Since in a demonstration a proper attribute is proved of a subject through a middle which is the definition, it is required that the first proposition (whose predicate is the proper attribute, and whose subject is the definition which contains the principles of the proper attribute) be *per se* in the fourth mode, and that the second proposition (whose subject is the

subject itself and the predicate its definition) must be in the
first mode. But the conclusion, in which the proper attribute is
predicated of the subject, must be *per se* in the second mode.
(In PA I.13.3)[29]

These requirements may be schematized as follows:

Subject's definition	is	*per se* attribute	(fourth mode)
Subject	is	subject's definition	(first mode)
Subject	is	*per se* attribute	(second mode)

For example:

The rational animal	is	risible
Man	is	the rational animal
Man	is	risible

Scientia is certain because it concerns what belongs *per se* to a
subject. Definitions are formulations of *per se* belonging, thus a
demonstration must use the definition of its subject as its middle in
order to explain the cause of an attribute's belonging (In PA II.1.9),
for only then can one be certain that the predicate belongs essentially to the definition of the subject and hence to the subject. Since
the middle must be a definition of the subject, Aquinas pauses at
Aristotle's demonstration that high and low notes are concordant
on the grounds that it uses the definition of a proper attribute as
its middle (In PA II.1.9). To explain this discrepancy, Aquinas relies
on the fact that scientifically demonstrated conclusions can form
the premises of further scientific demonstrations (In PA I.4.14). In
this case, the attribute signified through the middle has itself been
demonstrated to hold of the subject in a scientific demonstration
that uses the definition of the subject as its middle. Accordingly, we
already know that the attribute is essential to the subject and thus
that the predicate term of the latter syllogism also belongs essentially to the subject. The demonstration that established that the
middle term of the second demonstration is essential to the subject
is as follows:

Notes acting on the sense for a long and a short time are notes between which there is a numerical ratio.

Low and high notes act on the sense for a long and a short time, respectively.

Therefore, the low and high notes are notes between which there is a numerical ratio.[30]

The minor's formulation of the subject's definition is a statement of the first type of *per se* belonging; the major proposes the fourth type, as a numerical ratio exists between notes acting on the senses for various amounts of time owing to the type of notes they are. Finally, the conclusion illustrates the second type of *per se* belonging; for the definition of 'notes between which there is a numerical ratio,' incorporates 'low and high notes.' The definition must run: 'Notes between which there is a numerical ratio are high and low notes that concord,' insofar as 'concordance is a numerical ratio of high and low [*consonantia est ratio in numeris acuti et gravis*]' (In PA II.1.8).

From a demonstration employing the definition of low and high notes as its middle we arrive at a proper attribute of low and high notes. This proper attribute, in turn, can function as a middle in a demonstration uncovering more essential attributes of low and high notes, because whatever belongs essentially to a subject's proper accidents must belong to the subject as well.

Recall the demonstration that gave Aquinas pause:

Notes possessing a numerical ratio are concordant.

These high and low notes possess a numerical ratio.

Therefore, these high and low notes are concordant.

This demonstration uses the definition of a proper attribute as its middle. Yet it is acceptable because the attribute, 'possessing a numerical ratio,' was discovered to belong *per se* to the subject, 'high and low notes,' owing to the definition of high and low notes as notes that 'affect us for different lengths of time.' Moreover, this demonstration makes the requisite assertions of *per se* belonging outlined at In PA I.13.3. Although strictly speaking, 'possessing a

numerical ratio' is a proper accident of 'high and low notes,' the
former is nonetheless entailed by the definition of the latter. The
major can be taken to assert the fourth type of *per se* belonging
which requires nothing more than that the attribute in question
is attributed to a thing owing to itself (In PA I.10.7). Finally, the
conclusion asserts the second type of *per se* belonging, as we have
seen that 'concordance' is definable in terms of 'high and low
notes.'

*

Aquinas believes *scientia* is necessarily true and appears to hold
that God's existence is scientifically demonstrable. At the least,
such a demonstration must avoid the fallacy of equivocation but
it is unclear how Aquinas can manage this. His demonstrations
begin with observations pertaining to ordinary phenomena and
conclude with God's existence. In the context of a formal scientific
demonstration this would seemingly produce a syllogism whose
premises refer to one thing and whose conclusion seemingly refers
to another. Yet this is merely another instance of the difficulty that
confronts any attempt to learn of the creator through creation, as in
each instance we must begin with knowledge taken from creatures
and finish with statements about God, and we have already seen
that Aquinas believes that we can do this. He secures the veracity
of our knowledge of God with the claim that terms imposed to
signify creaturely attributes conceive God in a befitting manner
when we acknowledge the limitations his supereminence imposes
on the accuracy of our concept (SCG I.30); as a result the terms
that signify these ideas are analogical. Thus our understanding of
creaturely attributes and perfections informs us of God's attributes
and perfections, provided one accounts for God's supereminence.
With this in mind, Chapter 3 argues that Aquinas's Five Ways
use analogy of attribution to formulate scientific demonstrations
of God's existence that conform to the model of the scientific
syllogism discussed in this chapter.

Chapter 3

Scientia, Analogia, and the Five Ways

Aquinas claims God's existence is 'capable of being scientifically known and demonstrated [*demonstrabile est et scibile*].'[1] A scientific demonstration discerns what belongs to a thing because of its essence or nature, which is viewed as a cause with respect to the individual.[2] For this reason scientific knowledge (*scientia*) yields apodictic certainty with respect to individuals only inasmuch as these individuals belong to natural kinds (with natural kinds conceived broadly to take in phenomena such as eclipses). Yet, 'there can be nothing caused in God' (ST Ia.3.6c). Consequently, if God is an object of scientific knowledge, he is an object unlike any other, and Aquinas's demonstrations need to account for this.

Aquinas cites several reasons why nothing in God is caused, including God's being pure actuality and identical with his existence (ST Ia.3.6c). These are the same difficulties that lead Aquinas to claim that all talk of God is analogical. This gives two reasons to apply the parameters of analogy of attribution to Aquinas's Five Ways: (1) Aquinas says all talk of God is analogical, and the Five Ways talk of God; (2) Aquinas can no more literally say that God is a cause with respect to himself than he can say that God is good, yet analogy of attribution equips Aquinas to make the latter assertion and may likewise accommodate the former.

Scientia

For Aquinas paradigmatic scientific knowledge is rendered through syllogisms whose middle terms define the demonstration's subject (In PA I.13.3). If the definition is real, the definition is given in

terms of genus and specific difference and the demonstration
is termed '*propter quid*' (literally 'on account of the what'), its
conclusion necessitated by the nature (or *quiddity*) of the subject.
Here the nature furnishes the reason we ascribe the predicate to
the subject. On the other hand, *scientia* also uses nominal definitions where the subject is given a name (*nomen*) drawn from effects
proper to its essence. This proper name takes the place of a real
definition. However, if the effect is only accidentally connected to
the subject the effect is not proper and the demonstration from
the effect is not scientific. In contrast to *propter quid* demonstration
that accounts for effects through knowledge of the nature of their
cause, demonstration that relies on nominal definition is termed
demonstration '*quia*' (or demonstration 'that') and relies on effects
to disclose information about their cause (In PA II.1.8).[3]

Owing to God's absolute simplicity, there is no real definition
of God (ST Ia.3.5c). Thus scientific knowledge of God must
emerge from nominal definitions of the divine nature, i.e., by
means of effects proper to God. Moreover the difference between
creator and creation necessitates that the demonstrations' terms be
analogical.

Scientia and Divine Simplicity

Complexity involves what Aquinas terms 'potentiality (*potentia*),'
for complex things are potentially other than they are (ST Ia.3.7c &
ad 1). When what is in potentiality to F becomes F, it is said to be in
actuality (*in actu*) with respect to F. This actualization requires an
agent, for 'whatever is in potentiality can be reduced into actuality
only by some being in actuality' (ST Ia.3.1c). But if there is no being
that is pure actuality, an infinite regress emerges—which, for the
sake of argument, let us assume to be impossible[4]—since we would
lack a first actualizing cause that sets the others in motion. 'God'
is the name given this being who is pure actuality and altogether
simple (ST Ia.3.1 & 7).[5]

Aquinas attaches great significance to God's pure actuality.
Owing to his pure actuality God is not a body, seeing that bodies

are in potentiality to division (ST Ia.3.1c). Thus God is not other than his *suppositum*, which is the essence or nature that underlies what is said of him (ST Ia.3.3c). Furthermore being pure actuality God's essence does not stand in potentiality to his existence, meaning that he could not have been made (ST Ia.3.4c). God is his existence and thus a purely subsistent, necessarily existent entity. We have no direct experience of the divine nature, hence Aquinas adduces nominal definitions in support of his arguments for God's existence (ST Ia.3.5c).[6]

Analogia

Creation bears an imperfect resemblance to the creator owing in part to God's utter simplicity, for 'all perfections existing in creatures divided and multiplied pre-exist in God unitedly' (ST Ia.13.5c). Analogy of attribution must account for the imperfect manner in which creatures imitate the creator and thus Aquinas describes the relationship between God and creatures in terms of that which holds between medicine and a patient, the former being denominated 'healthy' owing to its ability to produce a state of health. The example originates in Aristotle's discussion of the notion of focal meaning,[7] the progenitor of medieval theories of analogy. In this context the example is unfortunate, for it suggests that God causes but is not characterized in terms of what is best in creation (an interpretation that Aquinas attacks [ST Ia.13.6c]), which would render theological discourse meaningless. Aquinas thus notes that God's names signify more than his activity as creator; ultimately everything depends on God for its existence, but were it the case that divine names signified only dependence there would be no reason 'why some names more than others should be applied to God' (ST Ia.13.2c). Thus, 'when we say, "God is good," the meaning is not, "God is the cause of goodness," or, "God is not evil"; but the meaning is "whatever good we attribute to creatures, pre-exists in God," and in a higher way' (ST Ia.13.2c). However, this optimism is tempered with a negative theology that leads Aquinas to assert that God is signified only through negation

(SCG I.30.4). It appears Aquinas interprets this stipulation as a denial of our ability to attain definitional or *quidditative* knowledge of God[8] owing to the unity in diversity of his essence (ST Ia.4.2, arg. 1), and this leaves room for positive knowledge of God that takes account of his supereminence (SCG I.30). These considerations suggest the following reading of Aquinas's analogy of attribution:

> A term '*F*' is analogical when *F* may be predicated of a subject '*x*' for one of two distinct though related reasons: either (1) (a) *x* possesses *F* in the highest possible degree, (b) is wholly identical with *F*, and (c) is the cause of other things less properly termed '*F*'; or else (2) *x* is itself that of which '*F*' is less properly said because (a) *x* does not possess *F* in the highest possible degree, and (b) *x* is not identical with *F*.[9]

In this way,

> Whatever is said of God and creatures is said in accordance with the fact that there is some ordering of creatures in relation to God, as to the principle and cause in which all perfections of things pre-exist more excellently. And this mode of participation is the middle between pure equivocation and simple univocation. (ST Ia.13.5c)

An elaboration of this reading will emerge as we consider the status of the Five Ways as scientific.

The Five Ways as Scientific Demonstration

The language with which Aquinas introduces his Five Ways suggests that he means them to be scientific demonstrations:

> There is nothing to prevent a man, who cannot grasp a proof [*demonstrationem*], accepting, as a matter of faith, something which in itself is capable of being scientifically known [*scibile*] and demonstrated. (ST Ia.2.2, ad 1)[10]

Note the presence of '*scibile*' and '*demonstrationem*'. Aristotle defines a demonstration ($\overset{\text{'}}{\alpha}\pi\acute{o}\delta\varepsilon\iota\xi\iota\varsigma$) as 'a scientific deduction [$\sigma\upsilon\lambda\lambda o\gamma\iota\sigma\mu\grave{o}\nu$ $\overset{\text{'}}{\varepsilon}\pi\iota\sigma\tau\eta\mu o\nu\iota\kappa\acute{o}\nu$], [i.e.] ... one in virtue of which, by having it, we understand [$\overset{\text{'}}{\varepsilon}\pi\iota\sigma\tau\acute{\alpha}\mu\varepsilon\theta\alpha$] something' (*An.Post* I 2, 71ᵇ17, trans. Barnes = In PA I.4). The thirteenth century possessed four Latin translations of Aristotle's *Posterior Analytics*, and Aquinas used at least two of these.[11] In each of the four, the translator selects '*demonstrationem*' for Aristotle's '$\overset{\text{'}}{\alpha}\pi\acute{o}\delta\varepsilon\iota\xi\iota\nu$' and some form of '*scire*' for '$\overset{\text{'}}{\varepsilon}\pi\iota\sigma\tau\acute{\eta}\mu\varepsilon\theta\alpha$.'[12] Accordingly, the technical sense of Aquinas's terminology is well established at the time he composed the introduction to his Five Ways, and it would be surprising were he to use '*scibile*' in a loose sense when introducing the *sine qua non* of natural theology, viz., proof of God's existence.[13] Moreover, scientific demonstration is intended to furnish necessary knowledge, and at the beginning of the Question where Aquinas presents the Five Ways he claims the proposition 'God exists' is true by definition once one grasps the meaning of its terms via a demonstration of the type he intends to furnish: 'I say that this proposition, *God exists*, of itself is self-evident, for the predicate is the same as the subject, because God is his own existence as will be hereafter shown' (ST Ia.2.1.c). Aquinas prefaces his Five Ways with the claim that their conclusions are true by definition and scibile. These claims justify (and even encourage) a reading of the proofs as scientific demonstrations.

The Five Ways

The Five Ways rely on five observations: things are in motion, there exists an order of efficient causes where one entity moves another, contingent entities exist, among beings we find varying degrees of perfection, and unintelligent entities exhibit seemingly end-directed activity. Aquinas argues that these phenomena disclose the existence of a first mover, first efficient cause, etc., and identifies these entities with God. Yet the existence of these explanatory beings[14] does not immediately point to the existence of the Christian God. Why should these entities possess God's perfections? Again, if God is the subject of each proof this seems to vitiate the demonstrations, for in God nothing is caused and scientific demonstration relies on *per se* causality. In what follows, I trace the path that Aquinas follows from the existence of these explanatory beings to that of God and consider how analogy of attribution may furnish a way to ascribe *per se* causality to the divine essence.

The First Way

> It is certain, and evident to our senses, that in the world some things are in motion. Now whatever is moved is moved by another, for nothing can be moved except it is in potentiality to that towards which it is moved; whereas a thing moves inasmuch as it is in act. For motion is nothing else than the reduction of something from potentiality to actuality. But nothing can be reduced from potentiality to actuality, except by something in a state of actuality. Thus that which is actually hot, as fire, makes wood, which is potentially hot, to be actually hot, and thereby moves and changes it. Now it is not possible that the same thing should be at once in actuality and potentiality in the same respect, but only in different respects. For what is actually hot cannot simultaneously be potentially hot; but it is simultaneously potentially cold. It is therefore impossible that in the same respect and in the same way a thing should be both mover and moved, i.e., that it should move itself. Therefore, whatever is moved must be moved by another. If that by which it is moved be itself moved, then this also must needs be moved by another, and that by another again. But this cannot go on to infinity, because then there would be no first mover, and consequently, no other mover; seeing that subsequent movers move only inasmuch as they are moved; as the staff moves only because it is moved by the hand. Therefore it is necessary to arrive at a first mover, moved by no other; and this everyone understands to be God. (ST Ia.2.3c)

The First Way as *Scientia*

The First Way investigates the phenomenon of motion to prove the existence of its ultimate cause: a first, unmoved mover whom Aquinas identifies as God. To evaluate its status as scientific we must cast it as a syllogism. The conclusion furnishes 'first mover' and 'exists' as our minor and major, respectively. Initially our knowledge of the first mover derives from experience. We see that things are moved. Aquinas understands motion as the reduction of potentiality to actuality. Consequently nothing is both moved and mover 'in the same respect and in the same way,' for were a thing to move itself in this manner it would actually have to be what it is only potentially. Yet if all that is moved is moved by another we face an infinite regress of moved movers. It is not that Aquinas denies the possibility of an infinite chain of movers each moving another whose subsequent activity as a mover is independent of the previous mover's. Rather Aquinas believes that the continual activity of a first mover is required to account for the existence of motion. He provides the example of a hand drawing a line with a stick; were the hand to cease moving the line would cease to be drawn (ST Ia.2.3c). So too a first mover is ultimately responsible for the activity of the planets, which are movers with respect to the sublunary realm (ST Ia.115.3, ad 2). This first mover is known to be ultimately responsible for motion, thus 'ultimate cause of motion' may serve as our demonstration's middle.

This provides the following schematism of the First Way:[15]

The ultimate cause of motion exists.
The first mover is the ultimate cause of motion.
Therefore, the first mover exists.

The major of a scientific syllogism must assert the fourth type of *per se* belonging (In PA I.13.3), thus existence must belong to the ultimate cause of motion owing to what it is (In PA I.10.7). We know that the cause of motion is itself 'moved by no other' and this suggests its pure actuality, for things that are moved are moved only insofar as they are in potentiality to that toward which they are moved (ST Ia.2.3c). Hence, what cannot be moved cannot be in potentiality, otherwise it would be movable. A being that is pure actuality exists necessarily as it cannot be other than the existence which it is through its very nature (otherwise this being would stand in potentiality toward non-existence). Accordingly, the major premise of our demonstration is an instance of the fourth type of *per se* belonging; the cause of motion exists *per se* or owing to its nature.

For its part, the minor premise of a demonstrative syllogism must assert the first type of *per se* belonging (In PA I.13.3), which our syllogism does, as 'cause of motion' is a nominal definition of 'first mover.'

Finally, the conclusion must assert the second type of *per se* belonging (In PA I.13.3), and if it does the conclusion should present existence as a *per se* accident of the first mover (In PA I.10.4). Temporarily setting aside what it means to refer to existence as a *per se* accident, let us first note that the first mover is God and God does not possess any *per se* accidents:

> Neither can he have any essential [i.e., *per se*] accidents ... Because such accidents are caused by the constituent principles of the subject. Now there can be nothing caused in God ... Hence it follows that there is no accident in God. (ST Ia.3.6c, brackets mine)

Thus strictly speaking, God cannot be the subject of a *per se* predication of the second type. In point of fact, God should not be able to be the subject of any *per se* predication that is productive of *scientia*, seeing that these predications assume that a subject acts on itself through principles simultaneous with it. Yet, *scientia* relies on such *per se* predications and this means that the considerations that rule against God's being the subject of a predication of the second type of *per se* belonging implicate as well all knowledge of what belongs *per se* to God, and with that all *scientia* of God.

Aquinas develops analogy of attribution to secure the project of natural theology, understood as an attempt to discern something of God's essence solely through reason (thus forgoing such avenues as Scripture or illumination). The need for analogy arises from the epistemic gap between God and creatures, and in the Five Ways this distance threatens reason's ability independently to verify Scripture's claim that God exists. Certainly Aquinas's comments in his earlier *Summa contra gentiles* suggest he allows for this delimitation of reason, for he prefaces his demonstration of God's existence as follows:

> There are certain likely arguments that should be brought forth in order to make divine truth known. This should be done for the training and consolation of the faithful, and not with any idea of refuting those who are adversaries. For the very inadequacy of the arguments would rather strengthen them in their error, since they would imagine that our acceptance of the truth of faith was based on such weak arguments. (SCG I.9.2)

However, this text should be weighed against Aquinas's belief that a demonstration of God's existence is central to the project of natural theology (SCG I.9, n. 5) and his aforementioned claims that he will demonstrate the necessity of the proposition 'God exists' (ST Ia.2.1c) and that this proposition is 'scientifically knowable (*scibile*)' (ST Ia.2.2, ad 1). Proceeding with the thesis that Aquinas allows for scientific demonstration of God's existence and that this is what he furnishes with his Five Ways, what follows explores how analogy of attribution enables him to do this.

The First Way as *Analogia*

On several occasions Aquinas asserts that God acts on himself through himself or *per se*, for example:

- God alone has every kind of perfection by his own essence [*secundum suam essentiam*] (ST Ia.6.3c).
- Since, then, God is not composed of matter and form [*cum Deus non sit compositus ex materia et forma*] he must be his own Godhead, his own life, and whatever else is so predicated of him (ST Ia.3.3c).

- God understands himself through himself [*per seipsum*] (ST Ia.14.2c).

The question is how (not whether) Aquinas's understanding of analogy of attribution allows for these ascriptions, assuming we take Aquinas at his word when he claims that all theological discourse is analogical (SCG I.34). Recall the suggestion that a term '*F*' is said analogically of God when God (a) possesses *F* in the highest possible degree, (b) is wholly identical with *F*, and (c) is the cause of other things less properly termed '*F*.'

As creator, God is the ultimate reason that creatures are able to act on themselves *per se*. This fulfills requirement (c). Again, God is pure actuality and thus utterly simple and identical with his immanent activity of *per se* causality, which he possesses in the highest possible degree, fulfilling (a) and (b). The link between pure actuality and the degree to which God possesses any attribute emerges in Aquinas's discussion of God's goodness, where God's goodness is termed 'highest' in part because God is good through his essence (SCG I.41.3), the latter ascription being deduced from his simplicity (SCG I.38.6), which is a result of his pure actuality (SCG I.18). Thus God may be termed a *per se* cause with respect to himself within the parameters of analogy of attribution.

Aside from its tacit reliance on *per se* causality, Aquinas's First Way predicates 'existence' and 'ultimate cause of motion' of its subject. The ascription 'cause of motion' is analogical if the first mover possesses this causality in the highest possible degree, is identical with it, and the cause of any other entity being less eminently named 'cause of motion.' Obviously the first mover makes other movers move other things and is thus the reason why any other mover is less eminently called a 'cause of motion.' That the first mover is nothing other than this causality is entailed by its being pure actuality, which also necessitates that the first mover's causal activity exists in the highest possible degree.

For existence to be analogically predicable of the ultimate cause of motion, it must be nothing other than its existence, existent in the highest possible degree, and the reason anything else is less eminently denominable as existent. The chain of reasoning by which Aquinas shows that God is ultimately responsible for all that exists allows us to conclude that the ultimate cause of motion is likewise responsible for all that exists; for Aquinas's argument that God is responsible for the existence of all else works from pure actuality, which the cause of motion has been shown to possess. First, as pure actuality God is immaterial (ST Ia.3.1c). The essence of an immaterial being is unique, seeing that this essence is not multiplied by matter (ST Ia.3.3c). Accordingly, there cannot be more than one God (ST Ia.11.3c), and he must be unique owing to his essence, which is identical with his existence (ST Ia.3.4). Yet, it is also the case that because he is pure actuality, God is essentially subsistent being, i.e., it is essential to God that he is necessarily existent (ST Ia.3.4c), and since his essence is unique, he is the only necessarily existent being (ST Ia.44.1c). Finally, as God is the only being whose existence is necessary, everything else merely participates in God's being and must therefore be caused by God; thus there is but one creator (ST Ia.44.1c; cf., SCG I.42). These inferences emerge from consideration of pure actuality, which Aquinas attributes to the first mover. Thus existence is predicable of the cause of motion within the parameters of analogy of attribution. Moreover, as the first mover is pure actuality we may conclude that it is identical with its existence, which it possesses in the highest possible degree.[16]

The Second Way

The Second Way is from the nature of efficient cause. In the world of sensible things we find there is an order of efficient causes. There is no case known (neither is it, indeed, possible) in which a thing is found to be the efficient cause of itself; for so it would be prior to itself, which is impossible. Now in efficient causes it is not possible to go on to infinity, because in all efficient causes following in order, the first is the cause of the intermediate cause, and the intermediate is the cause of the ultimate cause, whether the intermediate cause be several, or one only.

Now to take away the cause is to take away the effect. Therefore if there be no first cause among efficient causes, there will be no ultimate, nor any intermediate cause. But if in efficient causes it is possible to go on to infinity, there will be no first efficient cause, neither will there be an ultimate effect, nor any intermediate efficient causes; all of which is plainly false. Therefore it is necessary to admit a first efficient cause, to which everyone gives the name of God. (ST Ia.2.3c)

The Second Way observes the phenomenon of a series in which one entity is a partial cause of another's existence, the first entity's existence being temporally prior to the latter's. Human generation is one such series. One may conceive of this series as stretching back to eternity,[17] and Aquinas acknowledges this possibility (ST Ia.46.2, ad 7). Thus his comment that 'in efficient causes it is not possible to go on to infinity' may generate some puzzlement. If he elsewhere acknowledges that the series of generators can go backward into eternity, why does he seemingly adduce the opposite of this principle in support of the Second Way? The key to understanding this demonstration lies in the distinction between a *per se* and *per accidens* causal series. Thus far, '*per se*' has referred to the causality that a thing exercises of itself, owing to its nature. This is not how '*per se*' is used when Aquinas speaks of a *per se* ordered series. In such a series, the production of an effect is traceable to an ongoing activity, as the action of a stick moving a stone depends on the ongoing activity of what is moving the stick. Unlike a series ordered *per accidens*, a series ordered *per se* cannot proceed backwards to infinity:

In efficient causes it is impossible to proceed to infinity *per se*. Thus, there cannot be an infinite number of causes that are *per se* required for a certain effect; for instance, that a stone be moved by a stick, the stick by the hand, and so on to infinity. But it is not impossible to proceed to infinity *accidentally* [*per accidens*] as regards efficient causes; for instance, if all the causes thus infinitely multiplied should have the order of only one cause, while their multiplication is accidental: e.g., as an artificer acts by means of many hammers accidentally, because one after the other is broken. It is accidental, therefore, that one particular hammer should act after the action of another; and it is likewise accidental to this particular man as generator to be generated by another man; for he generates as a man, and not as the son of another man. For all men generating hold one grade in the order of efficient causes—viz., the grade of a particular generator. Hence it is not impossible for a man to be generated by man to infinity; but such a thing would be impossible if the generation of this man depended upon this man, and on an elementary body, and on the sun, and so on to infinity. (ST Ia.46.2, ad 7)

Aquinas's first example is of a *per se* ordered series of efficient causes. Let x, y, and z be the things in this series, x's activity being responsible for the activity of y and z. In this *per se* series x is causing y to cause z, as the hand is causing the staff to move the stone. The members of the series act simultaneously to bring about the unfolding effect and thus the series is termed 'synchronic.' Should x, y, or z cease to act, the ultimate effect will cease to unfold. Should the stick break or the hand stop pushing, the stone will cease to move to the extent that its movement is determined by their influence.

Now, let x', y', and z' be the members of series ordered *per accidens*. This series is termed 'diachronic,' meaning that its members can act independently of their temporally prior antecedents, as a son can beget after the passing of his father. Thus the activity of z' does not depend on the concurrent activity of either y' or x'. Again, though the example of a son and a father suggests otherwise, no member of this series need be solely responsible for the existence of another, the criterion for membership seems rather to be cooperative production with respect to some particular effect, as a child results from the cooperative productive activity of a father and grandfather, though the two do not act in unison. Aquinas uses the example of a series of (apparently cheap) hammers performing a particular task, each one breaking shortly into the job. Each hammer hammers independently of its ruined antecedents, but each hammer in the series contributes to the ultimate effect. Aquinas refers to the members of a diachronic series as particular generators, presumably highlighting that fact that each can operate independent of the immediate activity of its predecessor. Inasmuch as man is a particular generator, his activity does not constitute a phenomenon capable of demonstrating God's existence, as present activity in a series ordered *per accidens* can be explained without reference to the concurrent activity of another agent. Yet though Aquinas believes that 'it is not impossible' for such a series to extend indefinitely backward in time, he holds that a *per se* ordering underlies the possibility of at least some series that are ordered *per accidens,* and in the Second Way Aquinas relies on this necessity to demonstrate the existence of a first efficient cause.

The Second Way does not specify how God's concurrent action allows for the existence of the series ordered *per accidens,* but we find a clue in Aquinas's comment that:

> It is not impossible for a man to be generated by man to infinity; but such a thing would be impossible if the generation of this man depended upon this man, and on an elementary body, and on the sun, and so on to infinity. (ST Ia.46.2, ad 7)

This alludes to Aquinas's belief that human reproduction is partially caused by the planets, which are ultimately influenced by God:[18]

> Matter is not of itself sufficient to act, and therefore it is necessary to suppose some active principle above these material dispositions ... Therefore, as the Philosopher says, it is necessary to suppose a movable principle, which by reason of its presence or absence causes variety in the generation and corruption of inferior bodies [*On Generation and Corruption,* II 10, 336ᵃ15]. Such are the heavenly bodies. Consequently, whatever generates here below, moves to the production of the species, as the instrument of a heavenly body: Thus the Philosopher says that 'man and the sun generate man' [*Physics,* II 2]. (ST Ia.115.3, ad 2)

On this view, human activity is influenced by the planets' phases. Aquinas cites this as the reason that astrologers are often successful in predicting the future, failing only when human freedom manages to overcome the planets' sway (ST Ia.115.3, ad 3). The planets, in turn, are acted on by angels (ST Ia.110.3c), who execute God's will. Thus, human generation falls into a series ordered *per se* which ultimately terminates with God as its first efficient cause.

The Second Way as *Scientia*

The observed order of efficient causes is a *per se* ordered series and thus requires an entity ultimately responsible for its existence, viz., the first efficient cause, to whom 'everyone gives the name God.' Nominally defining the first efficient cause as the author of the *per se* series of efficient causes, we may represent Aquinas's syllogism as follows:

The author of the *per se* series of efficient causes exists.
The first efficient cause is the author of the *per se* series of efficient causes.
Therefore, the first efficient cause exists.

In the Question following his Five Ways, Aquinas asserts that 'it has been already proved that God is the first being. It is therefore impossible that in God there should be any potentiality' (Ia.3.1c). Presumably this comment builds on what was revealed about the divine essence under the guise of first mover, first efficient cause, etc. The First Way shows that its subject is first with respect to motion; the Second Way, that its subject is first with reference to a *per se* ordered series of generators. The demonstrations describe their subjects as first because these explanatory entities act independently of extrinsic influences, which is to say that these entities are pure actuality (and thus we should say 'this entity,' as pure actuality entails unicity). Hence existence belongs *per se* to the demonstration's subject rendering the demonstration scientific, and the Second Way may be cast as a scientific syllogism.

The Second Way as *Analogia*

The Second Way names God as 'first efficient cause' and demonstrates that he must exist. The ascription of existence is analogically attributable to God in his role as the first efficient cause since the first efficient cause is pure actuality and a being that is pure actuality possesses its existence in the highest possible degree, is utterly simple and ultimately responsible for the existence of all else, as was shown in the preceding discussion of the First Way. So too the name 'first cause' is analogically attributable to God. Being pure actuality he is wholly characterizable in terms of this immanent activity and possesses it in the highest possible degree. Moreover, the first cause is itself the reason other entities may be thought of as first causes in a less eminent sense, for it causes entities to act as causes with respect to one another as the hand causes the stick to act as a cause with respect to the stone.

The Third Way

The Third Way is taken from possibility and necessity, and runs thus. We find in nature things that are possible to be and not to be, since they are found to be generated, and to be corrupted, and consequently, it is possible for them to be and not to be. But it is impossible for these always to exist, for that which can not-be at some time is not. Therefore, if everything can not-be, then at one time there was nothing in existence. Now if this were true, even now there would be nothing in existence, because that which does not exist begins to exist only through something already existing. Therefore, if at one time nothing was in existence, it would have been impossible for anything to have begun to exist; and thus even now nothing would be in existence—which is absurd. Therefore, not all beings are merely possible, but there must exist something the existence of which is necessary. But every necessary thing either has its necessity caused by another, or not. Now it is impossible to go on to infinity in necessary things which have their necessity caused by another, as has been already proved in regard to efficient causes. Therefore we cannot but admit the existence of some being having of itself its own necessity, and not receiving it from another, but rather causing in others their necessity. This all men speak of as God. (ST Ia.2.3c)

The Third Way infers the existence of an uncaused, necessary entity from the existence of contingent entities. Here Aquinas has in mind what we may call 'ontological' rather than logical necessity. The being that 'has of itself its own necessity' with respect to its existence is one that cannot be otherwise and thus cannot cease to be.[19] Necessary entities can be either material or immaterial: 'Neither immaterial things nor things whose matter is not receptive of another form, have potentiality to non-being, so that their being is absolutely and simply necessary' (SCG II.30.2). The matter of necessarily existent material entities (planets for example) is not receptive of another form 'because their forms equal in their perfection the total potentiality of their matter, so that there remains no potentiality to another form, nor consequently, to non-being' (SCG II.30.9).[20] On the other hand, immaterial necessarily existent entities such as angels are necessary because they lack matter's potentiality toward non-being (SCG II.30.9).

Aquinas clarifies what it means to lack potentiality to non-being by discussing three types of necessity. The first type of necessity pertains to entities that cannot cease to exist owing to the ordering of their principles in relation to the act of being (SCG II.30.9). Aquinas illustrates this necessity with reference to the planets and immaterial entities. The second type is the necessity that an essence or form exercises in its governance of matter. For instance, if a creature is human its organs tend toward a certain arrangement (SCG II.30.10).[21] Third is the necessity pertaining to entities 'from the order of their essential principles to the properties flowing [*consequentes*] from their matter or form' (SCG II.30.11). Aquinas's examples of this third type of necessity (that a human is necessarily capable of learning or an iron saw necessarily hard) suggest he may be using 'properties (*proprietates*)' to refer to proper or *per se* accidents such as the snubness of a nose. In all three cases necessity is consequent on form, with an entity acting as an ontological cause with respect to itself.

From the existence of corruptible entities, the Third Way demonstrates the existence of necessary entities whose necessity is caused by another (such as planets and angels). Though necessary, these entities ultimately depend on God for their existence, as he possesses 'power to give them being, or to cease pouring forth [*desinat ... influere*] being into them' (SCG II.30.3). Let us call these entities 'metaphysically contingent.'[22] In contrast to metaphysically contingent entities, God does not have his being through another.

The Third Way begins by demonstrating the existence of metaphysically contingent entities. Were there naught but corruptible entities, then there would have come a time when all entities had ceased to exist. Thus, even now, there would be nothing. This is 'absurd [*patet esse falsum*],' therefore, necessary entities exist.[23] Every necessary entity either has its necessity caused by another or not and the former case entails an unacceptable regress, therefore an absolutely necessary being exists.[24]

The Third Way as *Scientia* and *Analogia*[25]

The Third Way rests on the principle that some necessarily existent entities are metaphysically contingent. This entails the existence of a *per se* existent entity. As the proof's subject exists *per se*, the proof obviously makes the requisite assertion of *per se* belonging. The nominal definition of this entity as the cause of the existence of metaphysically contingent entities provides the middle.

*

The proofs we have studied exhibit important similarities. In each, Aquinas begins with a phenomenon whose necessary condition is the existence of an entity that is pure actuality (as *per se* necessary, the subject of the Third Way must be pure actuality, were it not we would be thrown back to an inadmissible infinite regress of metaphysically contingent entities). From this pure actuality, we may deduce the unicity of the demonstration's subjects and that each subject is itself the author of existence, though Aquinas postpones these proofs until he has explored the ramifications of pure actuality.[26] Moreover, in each proof the explanatory entity in question must be truly characterizable in terms of certain traits. For instance, the first mover must actually be the first cause of motion, itself wholly unmoved. Thus Aquinas allows for positive knowledge of God's essence, and in the Fourth Way he will conclude that God possesses every perfection. However, to function as first mover, etc., God must be pure actuality, and God's being pure actuality (and consequently utterly simple) necessitates that theological discourse account for the profound difference between creator and creation via analogy of attribution.

The Fourth Way

The Fourth Way is taken from the gradation to be found in things. Among beings there are some more and some less good, true, noble, and the like. But 'more' and 'less' are predicated of different things according as they resemble in their different ways something which is the maximum, as a thing is said to be hotter according as it more nearly resembles that which is hottest; so that there is something which is truest, something best, something noblest, and, consequently, something which is most being; for those things that are greatest in truth are greatest in being, as it is written in *Metaphysics* [I 1, 993ᵇ30]. Now the maximum in any genus is the cause of all in that genus; as fire, which is the maximum of heat, is the cause of all hot things. Therefore there must also be something which is to all beings the cause of their being, goodness, and every other perfection; and this we call God. (ST Ia.2.3c)

The Fourth Way argues from grades of perfection to the existence of what is most perfect. Specifically, the phenomena of goodness, truth, and nobility entail the existence of one entity that is best,

truest, noblest, maximally existent, and the cause of other entities
exhibiting varying degrees of any perfection whatsoever.

The Fourth Way may be reconstructed in five propositions:

(1)   Some things are more F than others.

(2)   The existence of things more F than others entails the
        existence of what is most F.

(3)   Thus, the existence of things better, nobler, and truer
        than others entails the existence of one entity that is best,
        noblest, and truest.

(4)   What is best, noblest, and truest has the most being.

(5)   What is best, noblest, truest, and has the most being is the
        cause of both the being and the perfections of all other
        entities.

As noted in Chapter 1, the medievals had scarcely any access
to Plato's writings. Nonetheless his influence entered Christianity
through figures such as Augustine and Pseudo-Dionysius the
Areopagite; and Aquinas's Fourth Way is clearly inspired by a
Platonic metaphysics which supposes that for certain universal types
and attributes there are eternal exemplars that are themselves the
perfect instances of these types as well as the reason that particular
individuals imitate or instantiate these types, with varying degrees
of resemblance to the original exemplars. Since hot things exist,
there is some hottest thing, as there is goodness, there exists
something that is best, etc. Claim (5) in particular echoes Plato's
statement that the form or idea of the good is responsible for the
existence and perfection of all other entities:[27]

> The idea of the good ... is indeed the cause for all things of
> all that is right and beautiful, giving birth in the visible world
> to light, and the author of light and itself in the intelligible
> world being the authentic source of truth and reason. (*Republic*
> 517b8–c4)

For his part, Aquinas maintains that truth is primarily a property
of propositions: There is truth if what the intellect combines is

combined in reality, but there is falsity if what the intellect combines when it understands or forms a proposition is not combined in reality (*Sententia super Metaphysicam*, IX.11.1914).[28] Yet, he distinguishes between what John Wippel calls 'ontological' and 'logical' truth.[29] In our experience, some things are more intelligible than others. On Aquinas's world view these varying degrees of intelligibility are the result of the fact that different entities possess varying degrees of being. What is more intelligible possesses more being, and hence more ontological truth, which we may define as the quality present in a being whereby it is grasped by the intellect.[30] That truth which is in the intellect, on the other hand, described as 'the conformity of intellect and thing' (ST Ia.16.2c), is logical or epistemological truth. Since, then, an entity's ontological truth is greater the more being it has, whatever has the most ontological truth is most existent. Thus what is best, noblest, and truest has the most being.

The Fourth Way as *Scientia* and *Analogia*

The Fourth Way demonstrates the existence of a maximally existent entity that 'is to all beings the cause of their being, goodness, and every other perfection.' Aquinas justifies this conclusion with the Platonic principle that 'the maximum in any genus is the cause of all in that genus.' Since then the subject of the Fourth Way is truest, best, and noblest, the principle that the highest within a genus is the cause of all else within that genus allows Aquinas to conclude that the Fourth Way's subject is the cause of goodness, truth, and nobility. Why though does Aquinas feel justified in moving beyond this ascription to the additional claim that the subject of the Fourth Way is the cause of any perfection whatsoever?

The basis for this move may be a link between goodness and existence. Just as every being is characterizable in terms of ontological truth, so too 'every being, as being, is good' (ST Ia.5.3c). This is because goodness is nothing other than being under its aspect as what is desirable (ST Ia.5.1c). But a thing is good or desired only insofar as it is perfect: 'Everything is said to be good so far as it is perfect; for in that way is it desirable' (ST Ia.5.5c).

The connection between being, goodness, and desire ensures that what is most existent is most good (or simply best) and thus most desirable. This, in turn, means that it is most perfect, or excellent, by which Aquinas means that it possesses every perfection:

> Every excellence in any given thing belongs to it according to its being. For man would have no excellence as a result of his wisdom unless through it he were wise. So, too, with the other excellences. Hence, the mode of a thing's excellence is according to the mode of its being. For a thing is said to be more or less excellent according as its being is limited to a certain greater or lesser mode of excellence. Therefore, if there is something to which the whole power of being belongs, it can lack no excellence that is proper to anything[31] ... God, therefore, who is his being, ... has being according to the whole power of being itself. Hence, he cannot lack any excellence that belongs to any given thing. (SCG I.28.2)

Since the subject of the Fourth Way is maximally existent, it is best and possesses every perfection in the highest possible degree (providing Aquinas with a justification of the claim that the Five Ways demonstrate the existence of the God of revelation rather than mere explanatory entities). This being the case, by the Platonic principle that 'the maximum in any genus is the cause of all in that genus,' we have the reason that the first being is the cause of every perfection whatsoever.

The subject of the Fourth Way is most existent. To be most existent is to be pure actuality and thus the ontological ground of one's own existence. Accordingly, the conclusion of this demonstration is necessary. In the course of demonstrating the existence of the being that is the cause of the perfection and existence of all other beings Aquinas tells us this entity is best, truest, and noblest (henceforth simply 'best').[32] This supplies a middle for the following representation of the Fourth Way: What is best must exist and that which causes all others to possess existence and perfection is best, therefore the entity responsible for others' possessing existence and perfection exists.

The subject of the Fourth Way is best, existent, and causes others to possess existence and perfection. If analogical, these ascriptions signify this highest being as identical with its existence and perfections, as well as possessed of these in the highest possible degree and ultimately responsible for other entities' possession of these traits. This highest entity is most being, which is to say that it is pure actuality. Thus it is identical with these traits and possesses them in the highest degree. Finally, the entity ultimately responsible for other entities' existing and possessing perfections is likewise the reason that other entities are able to themselves cause others to exist or possess perfections.

The Fifth Way

The Fifth Way is taken from the governance of the world. We see that things which lack intelligence, namely[33] natural bodies, act for an end, and this is evident from their acting always, or nearly always, in the same way, so as to obtain the best result. Hence it is plain that they achieve their end not fortuitously. Now whatever lacks intelligence cannot move towards an end, unless it be directed by some being endowed with knowledge and intelligence; as the arrow is directed by the archer. Therefore some intelligent being exists by whom all natural things are directed to their end; and this being we call God. (ST Ia.2.3)

The Fifth Way reasons from the phenomenon of unintelligent things exhibiting seemingly end-directed activity to the existence of a supreme governor. By 'unintelligent things' or 'natural bodies' Aquinas likely has in mind elements, plants, heavenly bodies, and brute animals, which lack the capacity for intelligence.[34] First, he establishes that the behavior that they exhibit is actually end-directed and not the product of chance on the grounds that the behavior is persistent. This being the case, there must exist something that orders the activity, for unintelligent entities of themselves are incapable of acting for an end.

If one accepts Aquinas's reasoning, the question remains as to how Aquinas knows that there is an ultimate governor as opposed to several working in cooperation.[35] Moreover, if the activity of governance requires several agents, there is no reason to suppose that any one of these agents is pure actuality and thus able to possess its existence as a *per se* accident predicable of it in keeping with Aquinas's analogy of attribution. While I find nothing in the Fifth Way to secure the conclusion that its subject is unique or pure actuality, Aquinas elsewhere argues that what orders all things to their ends is an ultimate end or 'the first cause of all' (SCG III.17.9). The ultimate end is identified with the first cause of all on the grounds that there exists a hierarchy of ends, and 'the end holds first place over other types of cause' (SCG III.17.9). Within a hierarchy of ends, each end is posited for the sake of another. To avoid an infinite regress of ends, there must be an ultimate end, and as the end is the cause of causes—'for the agent acts only for the sake of the end' (SCG III.17.9)—the ultimate end is the first cause of all. As that for which all strive, the ultimate end is the highest good, and via the aforementioned connection between being and goodness, we may deduce this entity's pure actuality; for goodness is being under its aspect of what is desired, what is most desired is most good, and hence most being, and what is most being is pure actuality. Thus, creation is not ordered to multiple ends. There cannot be two ultimate governors because the ultimate governor governs through final causality and the ultimate final cause is pure actuality and hence unique.[36]

The Fifth Way as *Scientia* and *Analogia*

Existence belongs *per se* to a being that is pure actuality. Hence the demonstration is scientific, using 'cause of end-directed behavior in unintelligent things' as the nominal definition of its subject, who is 'some intelligent being by whom all natural things are directed to their end.' Owing to this entity's pure actuality, it is identical with its intelligence and immanent activity of governance, and possesses these characteristics in the highest degree. Moreover, as pure actuality (and thus the creator of all) the subject of the demonstration is the reason that other entities possess these traits in a less eminent manner. These considerations allow the demonstration to meet the requirements of analogy of attribution.

Conclusion

Each of the Five Ways accounts for certain phenomena by means of the activity of a being that is pure actuality. Though Aquinas does not always draw the conclusion that the subject of his demonstration is pure actuality, the logic of his proofs viewed in the broader context of his metaphysics demands it. In addition, each demonstration ascribes other perfections to this entity. This process culminates in the Fourth Way where Aquinas concludes that God possesses every perfection. This highlights the limits of the medicine–patient example as a paradigm instance of analogy of attribution. Unlike medicine which is denominated 'healthy' owing to an ability to produce some effect, God possesses the perfections he brings forth in creation.

Aquinas's natural theology attempts to map ideas drawn from creation onto the divine essence. Aquinas recognizes that the correspondence between the two is at best partial as creaturely perfections are contingent and separable from one another. Analogy of attribution preserves the content of ideas drawn from experience while allowing that when referred to God these ideas signify in an imperfect manner owing to God's supereminence.

Scotus shares Aquinas's desire to secure the veracity of theological discourse as well as Aquinas's appreciation that the distance between creator and creation challenges this effort. However, after rejecting prior and posterior signification—owing to skepticism regarding modistic speculation concerning the original imposition of terms significative in this manner—and also having rejected Henry of Ghent's theory of analogical predication, Scotus has to set out on his own to develop a way of balancing the competing demands of God's supereminence and our ability to attain knowledge of his essence. Scotus's theory of univocal predication answers this challenge by allowing that God and creatures are signified by technically equivocal terms with multiple, related significates that are united through a univocal core transcendental idea that refers equally to both God and creatures without any alteration whatsoever. Yet Scotus's claim that God and creatures are equally subsumed under transcendental ideas does not tip the scales in favor of reason, for God's infinite being renders him identical with his attributes and this unity in diversity forces an adaptation at the semantic level. While Aquinas insists that theological discourse account for God's supereminence, Scotus claims that transcendentals do not refer to God until joined with the notion of infinitude. Via these adaptations, both thinkers account for God's unity in diversity, mark off certain concepts as proper to God, and provide theological discourse with a meaningful link to ordinary language.

Chapter 4

Scotus and *Scientia*

Introduction

Scotus believes scientific knowledge (*scientia*) to be certain, yet he holds that different types of scientific propositions afford different levels of reliability.[1] Propositions such as 'a whole is greater than its parts' are true by definition and afford the highest level of certainty while *scientia* drawn from experience depends on the principle that 'whatever occurs in a great many instances by a cause that is not free, is the natural effect of that cause' (*Ord.* I, d. 3, pars. 1, q. 4, n. 234, *Philosophical Writings*, 109), meaning that certainty about the world is only as reliable as is experience. Yet God has the ability to upset the laws of nature, and even apart from divine agency experience is not wholly uniform, hence certainty about the natural world is not as reliable as that furnished through propositions true by definition. By contrast, though Aquinas believes that natural sciences cannot approach the certainty of sciences such as mathematics inasmuch as the former treat particular events, he nonetheless allows for scientific certainty about what pertains to extramental entities inasmuch as they belong to natural kinds (understood broadly to take in phenomena such as eclipses).[2] Thus we can attain truths about human beings in general but not about individuals. Scotus's thought developed after the Condemnation of 1277, which had the effect of emphasizing God's omnipotence,[3] and likely influenced Scotus's conception of scientific knowledge. Another influence may have been Scotus's rejection of Henry of Ghent's theory of illumination, which required Scotus to furnish an alternate explanation for our ability to attain certitude. Whatever the cause, Scotus's appraisal of *scientia* shows that he is more circumspect than Aquinas as regards the reliability of knowledge derived through experience.

*

Scotus understands Henry as claiming that we cannot attain certainty apart from divine illumination:

> [Henry maintains that] if man can know the infallible truth and possess certain knowledge it is not because he looks upon an exemplar derived from the thing by way of the senses, no matter how much such an exemplar may be purified and universalized. [Rather] it is necessary that he look upon the uncreated exemplar. And the way they assume this to take place is this. God does not function as exemplar in the sense that he is the object known so that unadulterated truth is known by looking at him. For God is known only under some general attribute. But God is the reason why we know inasmuch as he is the sole exemplar and the proper reason for the created essence ... When the uncreated light as it were illumines an intellect by a direct glance, then this light as seen is the reason for seeing the other things in it. In the present life, however, this uncreated light illumines our intellect indirectly as it were. Consequently, though unseen itself, it is the reason why our intellect sees. (*Ord.* I, d. 3, pars 1, q. 4, nn. 214–15, *Philosophical Writings*, 102)[4]

As noted in Chapter 1, Scotus believes this theory leads to radical skepticism: if illumination furnishes us with knowledge: of unchangeable realities it cannot provide meaningful insight into the unstable world in which we live; moreover, if the intellect requires an illumination to attain certainty, it is likely too weak to retain such knowledge.

In place of this theory, Scotus proposes that God designed the world in such a way that human beings are able to know his creation independent of an illumination:

The divine intellect, the true uncreated light, has a twofold causality ... It produces objects in intelligible being and ... it is also that in virtue of which the secondary objects produced actually move the intellect. (Ibid., n. 268, 125)

The 'objects in intelligible being' are God's ideas, exemplars after which creation is patterned. God's ideas are of all possible objects, any that ever exist as well as those whose existence is an unactualized possibility.[5] When these objects come into existence as intelligible things, this is owing to the activity of the divine intellect, 'for the divine intellect produces this intelligible in existence and by its act gives to this object one type of being and to another a second type of being' (ibid., n. 266, 124). Accordingly, as objects in creation are patterned after exemplars that God conceives as intelligible to human beings, we are able to know these objects without any direct illumination from God:

The divine intellect gives them such intelligible content as they possess as objects of knowledge. Now it is through their intelligible content that they afterward move the intellect to certain knowledge. And, properly speaking, it could be said that our intellect sees in the light, because the light is the cause of the object. (Ibid., n. 266, 124–25)

Since God invests objects with intelligibility he can be said to illuminate our minds. But unlike the the theory of illumination that Scotus attributes to Henry, illumination as understood by Scotus leaves us capable of attaining knowledge about things in the world because God conceives his creations as objects of human knowledge, and not because God chooses on each instance to allow it.

Certainty and Scientific Knowledge

Scotus identifies four 'kinds of knowledge of which we are necessarily certain' (ibid., n. 228, *adnotatio*, *Philosophical Writings*, 105), distinguishing one type as most certain because it does not rely on particular states of affairs but rather on relations among ideas. He outlines these four kinds of knowledge in a marginal annotation to his *Ordinatio* as well as in the text itself. What follows synthesizes the two accounts. In the text of the *Ordinatio*, Scotus considers three candidates for infallible knowledge:

> We must see ... whether it is possible to have infallible certitude naturally: (1) of self-evident principles and conclusions, (2) of things known by experience, and (3) of our actions. (Ibid., n. 229, 106)

In the annotation, (1) is revised and a fourth member is added:

> There are four kinds of knowledge of which we are necessarily certain, viz. (1) things knowable in an unqualified sense, (2) things knowable through experience, (3) our actions, (4) things known at the present time through the senses. (Ibid., n. 228, *adnotatio*, 105–06)

Here are the lists side by side:

	Adnotatio (**List 1**)	*Ordinatio* (**List 2**)
A	Things knowable in an unqualified sense (*scibilia simpliciter*)	Self-evident principles and conclusions (*principia per se nota et conclusiones*)
B	Things knowable through experience (*scibilia per experientiam*)	Things known by experience (*cognita per experientiam*)
C	Our actions (*actus nostri*)	Our actions (*actus nostri*)
D	One's current sense perceptions (*cognita a nobis ut nunc per sensus*)	

(2A) comprises propositions true by definition and the conclusions of demonstrations:

> The terms of self-evident principles are so identical that it is evident that one necessarily includes the other. Consequently, the intellect uniting these terms in a proposition, from the very fact that it grasps these terms, has present to itself the necessary cause, and what is more—the evident cause, of the conformity of this proposition with the terms that compose it. (Ibid., n. 230, 106–07)

Once we grasp the terms' definitions, the propositions require our assent:

> To give an example: If the notion of 'whole' and the notion of 'greater than' be taken from the senses and the intellect form the proposition 'Every whole is greater than its part,' the intellect by its own power and in virtue of the terms will assent to this proposition without the shadow of doubt. And it does not assent to this because it sees these terms verified in some thing, as it does when it assents to the proposition 'Socrates is white,' because it saw the terms united in reality. (Ibid., n. 234, 108–09)

Neither (2A) nor either instance of (C) (knowledge of our actions) rely on the senses 'because even if all the senses erred, there would still be certitude purely and simply' (ibid., n. 228, *adnotatio*, 106). In fact the certitude furnished by (C) resembles that attained via (2A), for knowledge of our actions 'is like that of self-evident propositions' (ibid., n. 239, 112); even if our perceptions are illusory 'still for all that there is certitude that I see even when the illusion is in the organ itself' (ibid.). Nonetheless (C) is of contingent states (Scotus uses the example of being awake), its objects are 'simply perishable' (ibid., n. 246, *adnotatio*, 112–13). Thus (C) cannot furnish the timeless truths on which demonstration relies.

Both instances of (B) (things known from experience) are known through the principle of the regularity of nature 'because a cause that does not act freely cannot in most instances produce an effect that is the very opposite of what it is ordained by its form to produce' (ibid., n. 234, 109). (1D) (sense perception), like (2A) (things known unqualifiedly) and (C) (actions), requires sense merely as an occasion, though it shares (B)'s reliance on the principle of the regularity of nature (ibid., n. 245, 115). Yet Scotus claims that on occasion this principle furnishes 'the very lowest degree of scientific knowledge—and perhaps we have here no knowledge of the actual union of the terms but only a knowledge of what is apt to be the case' (ibid., n. 237, 111). As for (1A), I argue below that (1A) and (2A) comprise one type of knowledge.

This breakdown of Scotus's lists suggests the following picture. (1A) and (2A) together constitute the most certain type of scientific knowledge. (C), while certain, does not generate the timeless truths on which *scientia* relies, and (B) and (1D) afford the lowest degree of certainty. Finally, the elevation of (1A) and (2A) results from Scotus's uncertainty regarding the uniformity of experience.

Self-Evident Principles

Medieval thinkers inherited their understanding of first principles, contained under (2A), from Aristotle who views them as the indemonstrable and better known premises from which scientific demonstration proceeds. For Scotus:

> Once we have certitude of first principles, it is clear how one can be certain of the conclusions drawn from such principles, since the perfect syllogism is evident, and the certitude of the conclusion depends solely upon the certitude of the principles and the evidence of the inference. (Ibid., n. 233, 108)

Aristotle recognizes two types of first principles, those particular to certain sciences and common principles known to all persons (*An.Post* I 32, 88ᵇ26–30); and within the set of principles particular to a certain science, some are assumed by the practitioners of that science while others result from demonstration (ibid., I 10, 33–36).

As noted in Chapter 2, common first principles are what 'it is necessary for anyone who is going to learn anything whatever to grasp' (*An.Post* I 2, 72ª17–18). Scotus's example of the proposition that a whole is greater than its part (*Ord.* I, d. 3, pars 1, q. 4, n. 234) is an example of a common first principle. The rules of inference are determined by these principles,[6] and different sciences use the principles differently, hence the principles are common to the particular sciences by analogy (*An.Post* I. 10, 76ª39–40). As Aquinas notes:

> Geometry does this [viz. adapt the common principles to its subject matter] if it takes the above-mentioned common principle [viz. that if equals be subtracted from equals, the remainders are equal] not in its generality but only in regard to magnitudes, and arithmetic in regard to numbers. For the geometer will then be able to reach his conclusion by saying that if equal magnitudes be taken from equal magnitudes, the remaining magnitudes are equal, just as if he were to say that if equals are taken from equals, the remainders are equal. The same must also be said for numbers. (In PA I.18.8).

Specific first principles, on the other hand, are unique to some one science, though they can be employed to prove the propositions of the subaltern sciences that fall under the science to which they belong, as the first principles unique to geometry are used to prove the propositions of optics (*An.Post* I 7, 75ᵇ16).

In a gloss on (1A), Scotus gives as an example of something known unqualifiedly the fact that the interior angles of a triangle equal two right angles (*Ord.* I, d. 3, pars. 1, q. 4, n. 228, *Philosophical Writings*, 106). This proposition is a demonstration from common and specific principles,[7] whose conclusion is elevated to the status of first principle and itself used to demonstrate that any triangle has its interior angles equal to the sum of two right angles: 'For example, if someone knows that every triangle has two right angles, he knows in a sense of the isosceles too that it has two right angles—potentially—even if he does not know of the isosceles that it is a triangle' (*An.Post* I 24, 86ª24–28). Therefore, since (2A) takes in both self-evident principles as well as conclusions and (1A) is illustrated by means of a scientifically demonstrable conclusion, (1A) and (2A) should comprise one class of knowledge.

Scientific Knowledge

First principles known in an unqualified sense and knowledge taken from experience make up two broad classes of scientific knowledge, and the former is more reliable than the latter as its truth is grounded not in experience but in relations between terms, or, more specifically, in necessary connections between their significates:

> The terms of self-evident principles are so identical that it is evident that one necessarily includes the other. Consequently, the intellect uniting these terms in a proposition, from the very fact that it grasps these terms, has present to itself the necessary cause, and what is more—the evident cause, of the conformity of this proposition with the terms that compose it. This conformity, then, the evident cause of which the intellect perceives in the terms, cannot help but be evident to the intellect. (*Ord.* I, d. 3, pars 1, q. 4, n. 230, *Philosophical Writings*, 106–07)

The certainty derived from the relations between the ideas signified by the terms of self-evident principles is assured even if the senses through which one initially takes these ideas be deceived:

> But will the intellect not err in its knowledge of [self-evident] principles and conclusions, if all the senses are deceived about the terms? I reply that so far as this kind of knowledge goes, the senses are not a cause but merely an occasion of the intellect's knowledge, for the intellect cannot have any knowledge of the terms of a proposition unless it has taken them from the senses. But once it has them, the intellect by its own power can form propositions with these terms. And if a proposition be evidently true by reason of the terms involved, the intellect by its own power will assent to this proposition in virtue of the terms and

not by reason of the senses from which it externally received the terms. (Ibid., n. 234, 108)

Thus a self-evident proposition is one the intellect knows to be true owing to its grasp of the proposition's terms. When terms render a proposition—more literally 'composition (*composito*)'— necessarily true, the composition is said to conform to the terms, and 'it is precisely this conformity of the proposition to the terms that constitutes the truth of a judgment' (ibid., n. 230, 107). Thus the proposition that a whole is greater than its parts is true regardless of any particular state of affairs; one need only grasp the meaning of the terms. This knowledge is certain no matter what, thus it is unqualifiedly certain. This account of certitude recalls Aristotle's conception of *scientia*:

> We think we know a thing absolutely ... whenever we think we are aware both that the explanation because of which the object is is its explanation, and that it is not possible for this to be otherwise. It is clear, then, that to know scientifically is something of this sort. (*An.Post* I 2, 71^{b}9–12)

Aristotle asserts that (1) unqualified scientific knowledge must be knowledge of a cause in its causality with respect to what is known, viz., its effect, and (2) it cannot be possible that what is so known be otherwise. Scotus appears to accept these criteria but grounds them in the signification of terms. The cause in its causality is a term's definition: 'It is evident that one [term] necessarily includes the other'; and what is known could not be otherwise because 'the intellect ... has present to itself the necessary cause' (*Ord.* I, d. 3, pars. 1, q. 4, n. 230, *Philosophical Writings*, 106–07).

Knowledge derived from the principle of the regularity of nature, on the other hand, is derived from effects that occur frequently owing to the nature of their subjects (ibid., n. 235, 110). Scotus initially describes this knowledge as infallible:

> As for what is known by experience, I have this to say. Even though a person does not experience every single individual,

but only a great many, nor does he experience them at all times, but only frequently, still he knows infallibly [*infallibiliter*] that it is always this way and holds for all instances. (Ibid., n. 234, 109)

Yet he allows that causes known in this manner do not always act predictably: 'A cause that does not act freely cannot *in most instances* produce an effect that is the very opposite of what it is ordained by its form to produce' (ibid., n. 235, 109). Thus we may be deceived by the principle of the regularity of nature and in such instances we have the weakest form of scientific knowledge, that is, such knowledge is not truly infallible:

We must be satisfied with a principle whose terms are known by experience to be frequently united, for example, that a certain species of herb is hot. Neither do we find any other prior means of demonstrating just why this attribute belongs to this particular subject, but must content ourselves with this as a first principle known from experience. Now even though the uncertainty and fallibility in such a case may be removed by the [principle of the regularity of nature] ... still this is the very lowest degree of scientific knowledge—and perhaps we have here no knowledge of the actual union of the terms but only a knowledge of what is apt to be the case. (Ibid., n. 237, 110–12)

*

A multitude of causes govern any particular event and our intellects are finite; this, together with God's ability to alter the course of nature, undermines the certainty of experiential knowledge. Though Scotus does not discuss the matter, his devaluation of experiential knowledge may likewise impact his estimation of Aristotelian natural theology. Transcendental terms conceive ideas of traits that belong to God. However, our understanding of these traits is only as reliable as the principle of the regularity of nature. At best, we know what is apt to be the case with respect to God, as our understanding of attributes such as goodness and wisdom is potentially open to revision in light of new experiences. Again, as

Scotus allows that it is difficult if not in some cases impossible to attain certainty about things in the world, he is unlikely to maintain that knowledge drawn from experience perfectly represents an entity we never directly encounter. Even setting aside issues that might arise in connection with the uncertainty that accompanies all experiential knowledge, talk of God must account for the unity in diversity that attends his infinite being (*De primo princ.* 4.75). For this reason infinitude seems to play a regulative role in transcendental signification, reminding us that concepts referred to God are abstract inasmuch as they conceive a simple entity via numerous isolated traits. Thus while knowledge of God may be reliable to the extent that any knowledge derived from experience is reliable, it dimly mirrors its object (*Quodl.* 14.91).

Chapter 5

Scotus on Naming and Understanding

Scotus believes that 'no name is able to be imposed on something more distinctly than it is understood,' meaning in part that we require some conception of a thing in order to name it.[1] Nonetheless we apply names to things we do not directly experience. This practice is especially evident in theological discourse; accordingly Scotus objects to an overly literal reading of the principle that naming follows understanding, for such an interpretation would leave us unable to say anything about God's essence.[2] Scotus advances his rejection of the literal interpretation as a criticism of Henry of Ghent, who (in Scotus's estimation) claims that we lack any names that accurately refer to God because we lack any direct experience of his nature. Against this, Scotus is convinced that experience provides positive knowledge of God's essence and he adduces this conviction (which is a prerequisite to Aristotelian natural theology) in support of his doctrine of univocity. Were we unable to learn of the creator from creation 'there is no more reason to conclude that God is formally wise from the notion of wisdom that we perceive in creatures than [there is to conclude] that God is formally a stone' (*Ord.* I, d. 3, n. 40, *Duns Scotus, Metaphysician*, 115).

Naming and Understanding: Aquinas and Scotus

Barring divine intervention, Scotus believes we have no direct experience of God, and accordingly no idea corresponding to such an experience (e.g., *Quodl.* 14.36; *Ord.* I, d. 3, pars 1, q. 2, nn. 56–57). Nonetheless, we know something of the divine essence through transcendental ideas arrived at via reflection and abstraction

(*Ord.* I, d. 3, pars 1, q. 2, n. 61). Though as noted in Chapters 1 and 4, this knowledge is incomplete since we cannot grasp how multiple attributes inhere in an essence with which each is identical, and it would seem likewise to be subject to the limits imposed on all experiential knowledge, which at best tells us what is apt to be the case (though Scotus does not explicitly connect this last difficulty with his discussion of the signification of theological discourse).

Yet as regards Henry of Ghent, Scotus believes that he denies our ability to attain any knowledge of God's essence. Scotus has it that Henry holds that God 'is not known from creatures, since a creature bears a remote likeness to him, for it resembles him only in those attributes that do not constitute this nature in particular' (*Ord.* I, d. 3, pars 1, q. 2, n. 20, *Duns Scotus, Metaphysician*, 140–41). In keeping with this denial that God is known from creatures, Henry stipulates we must rely on analogy to name God. Summarizing Henry on this point, Scotus notes:

> It is said that as God is understood by us, so also is he able to be named by us. In keeping with this, then [just as] people understand 'cognition of God by the wayfarer intellect' in different ways, so, consequently, they speak in diverse ways concerning the possibility of naming God. And he [viz., Henry] who denies a common concept, univocal to God and creature, and posits two analogous concepts (of which the one, derived from a creature, is attributed to the other, which is of God), will say in accord with this that God can be named by the wayfarer with a name expressing that analogous concept. (*Ord.* I, d. 22, q. un., nn. 2–3, trans. mine)[3]

From this point of view, we have no concept of God because we have no direct experience of the divine essence. Accordingly since the signification of terms derived from experience can never give an accurate picture of God's essence, Henry claims that theological discourse is analogical. However, Scotus charges that as Henry denies having any knowledge of God's essence, these analogical terms are ultimately uninformative and useless to the theologian (e.g., *Ord.* I, d. 3, pars 1, q. 2, n. 26).

Scotus's criticism of Henry's theory of analogical signification points to similarities between Scotus's and Aquinas's understandings of the signification of theological discourse. Both thinkers allow that experience provides a somewhat inaccurate though nonetheless informative picture of God's essence. For Scotus this manifests in his ranking our knowledge of God at the penultimate level on a scale comprising four grades of epistemic access to an entity's nature (*Ord.* I, d. 22, q. un., Appendix A). For Aquinas this leads to his denial that we can conceive God's essence in itself (that is that we have definitional knowledge of the divine essence) but must instead rely on the ways of excellence, causality and remotion discussed in Chapters 1 and 3:

> Since according to the Philosopher [*De Interpretatione* 1] words are signs of ideas, and ideas the similitudes of things, it is evident that words function in the signification of things through the conception of the intellect. It follows therefore that we can give a name to anything in as far as we can understand it. Now it was shown above [ST Ia.12.11–12] that in this life we cannot see the essence of God; but we know God from creatures as their cause, and also by way of excellence and remotion. In this way therefore he can be named by us from creatures, yet not so that the name which signifies him expresses the divine essence in itself in the way that the name *man* expresses the essence of man in himself, since it signifies the definition which manifests his essence [and we do not experience, and hence cannot define, God's essence].[4] (ST Ia.13.1c, brackets mine)

This chapter considers Scotus's estimation of our natural knowledge of God in light of his views on the relation between signification and understanding. Chapter 6 will explore how similar considerations shape Scotus's view of the signification of theological discourse.

Henry of Ghent's Account of Naming

Scotus's discussion of the relation between naming and understanding comes to us in part from his determination of the
question 'whether God can be named by us wayfarers with some
name signifying the divine essence in itself, as a "this" [*utrum Deus
sit nominabilis a nobis viatoribus aliquo nomine significante essentiam
divinam in se, ut est "haec"*]' (*Ord.* I, d. 22, q. un., n. 1, trans. mine).
The question as to whether God may be named as a 'this' asks
whether God can be named as a particular being, that is with
names proper (in the sense of being unique) to his essence.

As is often the case, Scotus's account develops in response
to Henry. Following the Condemnation of 1277 and the initial
disrepute it brought on natural theology in the broadly Aristotelian
framework, there was a reemphasis of the patristic tradition accom-
panied by a brief Augustinian revival.[5] This environment inspired
Henry to develop his theory of illumination with reference to
Augustine, who wrote that we arrive at knowledge of God's characteristics via a process of reflection that culminates with God
impressing this knowledge on us through an illumination.[6] Henry
interprets this passage as asserting that our reflection on creaturely
goodness (the attribute Augustine discusses) enables us to derive
an abstract idea of goodness. Then via reflection on this abstract
concept of goodness and through the aid of divine illumination, we
receive an idea of goodness that is related to but not a part of God's
essential nature. This new concept has a meaning that is different
from though very close to the initial concept, and Henry says that
the two concepts are analogous.

Scotus describes Henry's process of ascent in terms of a fivefold
approach to knowledge of God's being.[7] First, we grasp the concept
of being as it relates to creatures, this is to conceive God 'most
indistinctly.' Second, we conceive abstract being by taking away
particularity from the concept of being as it relates to creatures.
Next, through reflection on this concept and the aid of a divine
illumination, we come to distinguish between negatively and privatively indeterminate being, the former is proper to God and thus
incommunicable and unqualified, the latter has no existence apart

from particulars. In the fourth stage what is attributed to God is said to belong most eminently. Finally the fifth stage recognizes God's utter simplicity and identifies him with his attributes.

Scotus objects to Henry's theory for several reasons. On the one hand, as discussed in Chapter 1, Scotus rejects Henry's reliance on illumination on the grounds that (1) if knowledge received through illumination is of unchanging realities it would not refer to creation (at least not if creation is thought to be in flux, a position Scotus attributes to those he refutes); and (2) a human mind so weak as to require an illumination to know something of God's essence could not retain knowledge thus acquired. Over and above these difficulties, Scotus objects to Henry's claim that the ideas arrived at via illumination are not of God's essence but rather pick out what surrounds or is related to that essence:

> A certain teacher [viz. Henry] answers the question [as to the extent to which we can know God] in this way. Speaking of the knowledge of anything, one can distinguish on the part of the object known a knowledge that stems from the thing itself or from something accidental to it and knowledge in particular and in general. In reality God is not known through anything accidental, since whatever is known of him is himself. Nevertheless, in knowing some [proper] attribute of his, we know what God is in a quasi-accidental way. Hence Damascene says that the attributes do not assert the nature of God but things about his nature ... In particular he is not known from creatures, since a creature bears a remote likeness to him, for it resembles him only in those attributes that do not constitute this nature in particular. Therefore, since nothing leads to the knowledge of something else save by reason of a similar characteristic, it follows [that God is not known in particular through creatures]. (*Ord.* I, d. 3, pars 1, q. 2, n. 20, *Duns Scotus, Metaphysician,* 140–41, first and second brackets mine)

Henry discusses three ways of knowing God: through himself (*per se*), through his accidents (*per accidens*), or through his attributes (*de attributa*). God does not possess any accidents and we do not know his essence. This eliminates the first two, leaving knowledge of properties uniquely related to God's essence. Knowing these properties we know God in a quasi-accidental way. This suggests that these properties are conceived along the lines of proper accidents, dependent for their existence on a nature that is able to subsist without them after the manner that odd and even depend on number. In some respects, Henry's notion of the divine attributes resembles that ascribed to Aquinas in Chapter 3, where it was argued that Aquinas believes demonstration discloses what belongs *per se* to the divine essence. However, it was also noted there that Aquinas believes that this knowledge refers directly to God's essence. For his part, Henry (as read by Scotus) denies that knowledge of God's attributes tells us anything about God's nature.[8] Accordingly, on the principle that naming follows understanding and we have no understanding of God's essence, language cannot pick out the divine essence as a 'this.'

Scotus's Account of Naming

Scotus ultimately affirms that we can name God's essence as a this, but before advancing his opinion he argues against Henry's claims that (1) we can understand God's properties without understanding something of the divine essence, and (2) our notions of God are analogical. Here again is Scotus's summary of Henry's position:

> It is said that as God is understood by us, so also is he able to be named by us. In keeping with this, then [just as] people understand 'cognition of God by the wayfarer intellect' in different ways, so, consequently, they speak in diverse ways concerning the possibility of naming God. And he [viz., Henry] who denies a common concept, univocal to God and creature, and posits two analogous concepts (of which the one, derived from a creature, is attributed to the other, which is of God), will say in accord with this that God can be named by the wayfarer with a name expressing that analogous concept. (*Ord.* I, d. 22, q. un., nn. 2–3, trans. mine)[9]

The analogous notions that Scotus discusses are presumably Henry's negatively and privatively indeterminate concepts, the former are arrived at through illumination in the third stage of our ascent to knowledge of God while the latter are abstracted from creatures. Henry holds that an idea arrived at through abstraction from creaturely properties is attributed or ascribed to an idea we refer to God. The verb '*attribuere*' can mean simply 'to ascribe' but also connotes causality where one thing is ascribed to another because the former is an effect of the latter. Perhaps then this attribution recognizes the dependence of creaturely attributes on the creator. Be that as it may, Scotus objects to this account because the idea referred to God is different than that which refers to creatures as the former is not of God's essence but of attributes that lie about that essence. Owing to the close resemblance between concepts derived from creatures and those arrived at via illumination Henry says that these concepts are analogous. But, as Scotus is quick to point out, this notion of predication violates our understanding of proper attributes. A proper attribute is proper because its subject is its ontological ground. We cannot affirm that an attribute is proper while denying that it tells us something of its subject's essence, for then the proper attribute would simply be an accident. If we cannot grasp anything of God's nature, we cannot grasp any of the attributes that are proper to his nature:

> It is conceded that the wayfarer has some quidditative concept of God; this is evident, because otherwise he is not able to have any qualitative or relative concept of God. For the qualitative concept always requires something quidditative in which it inheres, but according to him [viz., Henry] a quidditative concept of God, common to God and creatures, cannot be grasped. (Ibid., Appendix A, 389, trans. mine)[10]

We possess qualitative and relative concepts of God. For instance we assert that God is good (a quality) and related to us as the creator. In the case of qualities such as goodness, Scotus believes they tell us something of God's essence; to say for example that God is good is to say something about God, not merely about some property encircling his essence.[11] Thus Scotus is certain that we know something of God's nature. To clarify the character of this knowledge (arrived at without any direct experience of the divine essence) Scotus considers naming in general and extrapolates from this an account of how we name what we never experience. He then considers differing levels of epistemic access to an entity's nature and locates our knowledge of God's essence on a scale comprising the grades he discusses.

Scotus's account of naming traces imposition to experience, which does not furnish direct knowledge of substances but can sometimes inform us of accidents that are essentially connected with different natural kinds. Accordingly, we impose names on things inasmuch as things are cognitively present to us by means of various properties that we grasp through understanding. The ability to signify a substance with a name drawn from its properties (either essential or purely accidental) allows us to signify substances more distinctly than they are understood:

> Since the wayfarer has no understanding of substance save in a common concept of being (as was proven in distinction three), if substance were not able to be signified in a more distinct manner than it is understood, no name imposed by the wayfarer would signify anything in the genus of substance. (*Ord.* I, d. 22, q. un., n. 5, trans. mine)[12]

The reason we do not conceive substance save in a universal concept of being is that our intellects are naturally moved by accidents rather than substances:

> Substance does not immediately move our intellect to know the substance itself, but only the sensible accident does so. From this it follows that we can have no quidditative concept of substance except such as could be abstracted from the concept of an accident. (*Ord.* I, d. 3, q. 3, *Philosophical Writings*, 5)

Yet despite the mediated quality of our knowledge we are able to signify different kinds of substances with a variety of names derived from experience: 'Just as some property (commonly expressed through the etymology of the name) from which a name is imposed is precisely conceived by the intellect of the wayfarer, so too is such a property precisely signified through the name' (*Ord.* I, d. 22, q. un., n. 5, trans. mine).[13] Accordingly, the names that we have for types of substances do not depend on a direct acquaintance with substance in order to signify substances. The name 'rock (*lapis*)' is one such term. Western medieval etymology (rooted in the *Etymologia* of Isidore of Seville) maintained that the name 'rock (*lapis*)' was imposed when a person striking a rock received an injury (*laesio*) to his foot (*pedis*). Thus the name '*la-pis*' actually combines the terms '*laesio*' and '*pedis*,' and means something like 'injury to the foot (*laesio pedis*).' Yet despite 'injury to the foot' belonging to the genus of action, '*lapis*' is the name of a substance, 'thus it may be argued concerning any other name imposed on things of the genus of substance that not one of them signifies anything other than some accidental property that was understood by the person imposing the name' (ibid., n. 6).[14]

When Scotus returns to the question as to whether we can name God with some name signifying the divine essence as a 'this,' his response relies on our ability to signify more distinctly than we conceive, that is our ability accurately to signify a particular type of being as a particular type of being, and not merely a being, through terms imposed on the properties through which the being is cognitively present to us. Hence despite our lack of direct experience of the divine essence, our conception of that essence as it is cognitively present through its effects is sufficient to warrant the claim that theological discourse conceives and can thus refer to God. Again turning to substances, we are aware of them through accidents and can distinguish one substance from another by attending to the different accidents that tend to cluster around different natures:

[Individual substances] are conceived through many accidents coming together in the same thing, for example, such a quantity and such a quality ... But [such a quantity and such a quality] are not joined together the same way in different subjects.[15] From the different way they are conjoined in different things, it is concluded that the substratum for some differs from the substratum for others, and from this that this [quality and quantity] differ from another third thing [viz., the substance in which both inhere]. But the name 'some thing' is imposed on this other [viz., the substance in which the quantity and quality inhere] as distinct [from another substance] … This seems to be the proper sign of this [substance], inasmuch as it is a 'this,' for when imposing the name, the name-giver intended to signify that essence from the genus of substance. And as he intended to signify, so the name he imposed is a sign. Nevertheless he himself does not distinctly understand that which he intends distinctly to signify through this name or this sign [as the name-giver conceives the accidents rather than the quiddity of a substance]. (Ibid., n. 7)[16]

Though substances are cognitively present only through their accidents, we are able to distinguish one type of substance from another because different types of substances are attended by different types of accidents, and the names of substances are taken from these different groupings of accidents. But name-givers do not intend that the terms they impose should signify nothing save accidents, instead they wish to signify the substances upon which these accidents depend for their existence, described as 'whatever it is which is joined with these [accidents], which are understood [*quidquid sit illud quod est cum istis coniunctis, quae intelliguntur*] (ibid.).

While signification follows understanding, a name that refers uniquely to one type of being does not depend on an ability to conceive an entity's quiddity. Accordingly Henry is wrong to adduce lack of direct contact with God's essence in support of the conclusion that we have no ideas that refer to that essence. Experience teaches us of God through his effects and 'many names are imposed which signify God in a commonly accepted manner, because it is in this way that he is able to be naturally conceived by the wayfarer' (ibid., n. 9).[17] Again, some of the divine names have been transmitted through God himself or the angels, and the fact that they do not signify a direct conception of God's essence does not stop us from accepting that they refer to that essence. In sum:

God can be named by the wayfarer with a name that properly signifies the divine essence as it is 'this [particular] essence' [and no other], because the wayfarer is able to use that sign and to intend to express the signification of that sign. Either he himself may impose that sign or some other who knows the signification. And the wayfarer is able to use such a sign or name just as a name, even if he was not able to impose that as a sign. And if this proposition is true that 'no name is able to be imposed on something more distinctly than it is understood,' this nevertheless is false that 'no one is able to use a name signifying a thing more distinctly than he himself is able to understand.' Accordingly, it absolutely must be conceded that the wayfarer is able to use many names that express the divine essence as unique from any other. (Ibid., n. 11)[18]

God may be named through names that are proper to the divine essence and hence pick it out as unique from all else. It remains to determine how informative these names are or what cognitive grasp of the divine essence our ability to use them entails. Accounts preserved from Scotus's lectures (given in Appendix A of the fifth volume of the Vatican edition) report him as claiming that our knowledge of God is no more informative than knowledge of some natural kind given solely in terms of its proximate genus; such would be the knowledge of a person who knew of *homines* (men) only that they were some type of animal.[19]

In this report (*reportatio*), Scotus's question is 'whether God is able to be named by the human wayfarer with some proper name [*utrum Deus sit nominabilis ab homine viatore, aliquo nomine proprio*]' (*Ord.* I, d. 22, q. un., Appendix A, 384, trans. mine), and a proper name is defined as 'any name that signifies something that is able to belong only to this [subject]' (ibid., 390).[20] Scotus adds that these names are termed 'proper' because they refer uniquely, not because they signify properties related to entities' essential natures: 'It is not a proper name of this absolutely speaking, except that the name primarily signifies this under a unique concept, because only that is a proper vocal sign of this' (ibid.).[21] In this context a name is proper to God if it refers solely to God, but one using such a name need not directly grasp the whole of God's essence.[22]

As in the *Ordinatio*, Scotus argues that God is named with proper names, understood as names that refer uniquely to his essence. But in the *reportatio* Scotus proceeds to locate God's names on a scale comprising four grades of epistemic access to an entity's nature, ranked in order from least to most informative, with the fourth type being the most perfect:

> Accordingly there is this order: to use the name [1] as such a thing; [2] as a conventional sign of something, of which, however, the one using the name has no concept (save in this most universal way, [viz.] that there is something signified by this name); [3] as a sign of something, of which the one using the name has only the universal concept (nonetheless he intends to express that which is signified through that name, although he does not conceive it in a particular manner); [4] as an expressive sign of a proper concept in particular. And here, the prior grade is always imperfect with respect to the posterior: Therefore, the first is most imperfect, the last absolutely perfect. (ibid., 391)[23]

To use a name as 'as such a thing' is to utter a name without being aware that it signifies. Scotus illustrates this kind of name use with the example of a bird trained to mimic human speech, as he believes that the bird mouths words without realizing that they mean anything. The second way that names are used is when persons utter names without grasping their signification, though they are aware that the names have some signification. For instance a Latin speaker who does not know any Hebrew may nonetheless utter Hebraic words. He knows that the terms are significative, but not what they signify.[24] Using a name in the third or fourth manner, however, one grasps something of the nature of that which the name was imposed to signify. Such a language user uses the name 'as the sign of a concept that has been inculcated through use [*ut signo conceptus habiti ab utente*]' (ibid., 390). Scotus gives as an example of the third type of name use a person who knows enough of the signification of '*homo* (man)' to realize that it picks out an animal, but does not realize that the term refers to human beings, i.e., to *rational* animals:

> He has a less perfect or confused concept, like one who only has the concept of animal uttering the word 'man,' intending to express ... through the name what others conceive through the name and what the name was intended to signify. He knows that he imposes on some species under animal, however, insofar as it is signified under this name, he does not know in particular what [he signifies]. (Ibid., 391)[25]

Finally, to use a name in the fourth manner is to use it perfectly. Earlier Scotus notes that one who uses a name in this manner 'grasps a concept that is proper just as the name signifies [*habet conceptum ita proprium sicut nomen significat*]' (ibid.). This locution may indicate that one who uses a name perfectly has a complete grasp of the essential nature of that to which he refers and fully conceives this nature by means of the term he uses, as one who uses the term 'human being' knowing that human beings are rational animals.

Next, Scotus applies these considerations to resolve the question as to whether we possess names that are proper to God in the sense that they refer uniquely to his essence:

> From what is said, the first conclusion pertaining to the question [of the distinction] is this: God is able to be named by the imperfect wayfarer by means of an absolutely proper name, in the third of the aforementioned grades. Second: It is not possible that God be perfectly named by the wayfarer, namely in accord with the fourth grade. Third: He is named by us as if from a fact. (Ibid.)[26]

The first conclusion is proven because we signify substances distinctly despite the fact that we lack any concept '*per se* and proper [*per se et proprium*]' to substance (ibid.). Scotus does not elaborate on his grounds for the second and third conclusions; however, his claim that we cannot perfectly name God may refer to his earlier comment that we are unable to form an intellection 'comprehensive of God [*comprehensiva Dei*]' (ibid., 388) owing to God's being infinite, which is not to say that we cannot form an intellection of God's infinitude:

> Every name is a finite sign, even if it is imposed by God on himself with respect to his immeasurability. Therefore, as it is a sign to some intelligence, it is not necessary that this [intelligence] have an infinite intellect. Therefore, a finite intelligence can name God with any name whatsoever. (Ibid.)[27]

Scotus's claim that God 'is named by us as if from a fact' may allude to God's being named from his effects conceived as facts that make us aware of his nature.

The report concludes with the following summary:

> Therefore, it is evident that the intellection from which a name is imposed is one thing (and the word's etymology signifies what this is), and what it is imposed upon is another. Thus, [in the case of naming in general] although the one imposing a name has no distinct concept save of the name, he does not impose the name on that intellection, but on the substance of which the intellection is a description, and this for some reason proper to that substance but unknown to ourselves. And consequently [when naming God] he names as one imperfectly imposing in accord with the third grade. (Ibid., 393)[28]

Naming follows understanding, nonetheless we can name more distinctly than we understand, meaning that names can uniquely signify entities that we do not directly encounter, including God. When a term signifies God, it conceives a transcendental characteristic joined with the notion of infinitude (*Ord.* I, d. 8, q. 3, n. 113). Our finite minds conceive infinitude imperfectly and this may be why we name God after the manner of a person who uses the term 'man' knowing only that human beings are some type of animal. This suggests that the conjunction of transcendentals with infinitude is more regulative than informative, with infinitude serving primarily to mark off the resultant complex concept as proper to God in a manner that recalls Aquinas's insistence that theological discourse must account for God's supereminence (SCG I.30.3), which is not to suggest that either thinker denies that we conceive attributes that truly belong to God, merely that each recognizes the importance of allowing for the distinction between creator and creation.

Scotus's discussion invites the comparison of our notion of infinitude to the specific difference by means of which a genus is contracted. Thus transcendentals prescinding from considerations pertaining to either finitude or infinitude would be akin to genera, with the notions of finitude and infinitude serving to narrow their extension, rendering them proper to creatures and God respectively. Now Scotus would never allow our concepts of infinitude and finitude to function as specific differences, as this would threaten to reify being into a genus above God and creatures, a move ruled out by Aristotle.[29] This leads Scotus to posit that the difference between God and creatures with respect to the transcendental attributes is one of degree, which threatens to bring God down to the level of creatures. Chapter 6 considers how Scotus navigates these difficulties and what impact this has on his understanding of terms that univocate both God and creatures.[30] Chapter 7 concludes the examination taken up in Chapter 6 and revisits the similarities between Aquinas's and Scotus's understandings of the signification of theological discourse.

Chapter 6

Scotus on the Signification of Theological Discourse

Scotus requires an account of signification that secures the veracity of theological discourse without ignoring the epistemic gap that separates the creator from creation, yet as noted in Chapter 1 he denies the existence of terms that signify in a prior and posterior manner (likely owing to his belief that primary signification is fixed).[1] For Aquinas, however, such terms signify differently in different contexts while retaining an order among their significates through which these significates have something in common. Aquinas uses this type of signification when he employs analogy of attribution to speak of God, allowing that analogical terms signify God as the cause of and identical with all perfections, which therefore may truly be said to belong to him, thus salvaging the veracity of theological discourse (SCG I.30). Having rejected prior and posterior signification, Scotus calls any term with multiple significates equivocal, whether or not the significates are related. On this model, any term said of God and creatures is equivocal, even 'being,' which Scotus tells us signifies three different though related ideas, dependent on whether one conceives infinite being (God), finite being (which pertains to creatures), or being prescinding from consideration of degree (*Ord.* I, d. 3, pars 1, q. 2, n. 29). However, the equivocity of terms with multiple related significates does not render them unfit for theological discourse. For the core transcendental signification through which these terms are related (in the example of being, being prescinding from consideration pertaining to degree) applies equally to both God and creatures while referring properly to neither until joined with the notion of infinitude or finitude, respectively.[2]

Transcendental terms signify ideas that concern 'whatever pertains to being … insofar as it remains indifferent to finite and infinite' (*Ord.* I, d. 8, q. 3, n. 113, *Philosophical Writings*, 2), thus transcendental ideas are of being *qua* being. As noted in Chapter 1, Scotus recognizes three types of transcendental ideas. First, he follows tradition in assigning goodness, truth, and unity to any being that exists. These make up the group of attributes coextensive with being. Second, are the transcendental disjunctions, each of which is a pair of attributes that exhausts the class of existent things, for instance, all beings are animate or inanimate, free or determined, etc. Finally, all entities are likewise characterizable in terms of certain pure perfections, defined as perfections that are unqualifiedly better than anything incompatible with them. The coextensive and disjunctive attributes together with the pure perfections round out the list of what pertains to all beings.

Transcendental terms signify ideas that pertain to being and hence are predicable of all existents. For instance, every entity is singular, possessed or not possessed of a will, better off were it wise, and, if unable to attain wisdom, better off were it transformed into something capable of being wise and then granted wisdom. The transcendentals signify a multitude of perfections and attributes and are a rich source of information about God, reflecting his image in creation.

Yet, if God is properly named with terms whose signification is derived from experience, what separates God and creatures? God is a being unlike any other, how then can he be named like any other? On the other hand, if God's being is different from that of any other entity, it appears that it must be different by some difference, in which case being would become a genus over and above God and creatures. Finally, if as Scotus argues the difference is one of degree, once again we must ask what it is that separates the creator and creation if the two are commensurable with respect to degree of being? On the other hand, if the two are incommensurable, how can Scotus argue that the difference is merely one of degree?[3]

*

Transcendentals signification is rooted in experience (*Ord.* I, d. 3, n. 40). Stripped of creaturely limitations, transcendentals form the nucleus of compound ideas predicable of God and creatures on the grounds that transcendentals belong to being *qua* being and thus pertain to God and creatures inasmuch as both are subsumed under the concept of being:

> Now a doubt arises as to what kind of predicates are those which are predicated formally of God, for instance, 'wise,' 'good,' and the like. I answer that before 'being' is divided into the ten categories, it is divided into infinite and finite. For the latter, namely finite being, is common to the ten genera. Whatever pertains to 'being,' then, insofar as it remains indifferent to finite and infinite, or as proper to the infinite being, does not belong to it as determined to a genus, but prior to any such determination, and therefore as transcendental and outside any genus. Whatever [predicates] are common to God and creatures are of such kind, pertaining as they do to being in its indifference to what is infinite and finite. (*Ord.* I, d. 8, q. 3, n. 113, *Philosophical Writings*, 2)

Being divides into ten categories, which between themselves comprise its finite manifestations. Prior to this division being divides into finite and infinite being. The priority here is merely logical; there is no subsistent, finite being that does not belong to any category. Rather, there is one infinite being, and ten categories of finite being (viz., substance and the nine accidental categories).[4] Infinite being and the ten categories comprise all that exists.

We arrive at our concept of transcendental being (i.e., being that is neither finite nor infinite) through abstraction, and joining this concept with notions of finitude and infinitude does not alter its signification:

> Someone, seeing that the philosophers disagree, could have been certain that what someone had proposed as a first principle was a being, and still, because of the contrariety of their opinions, could be in doubt whether [the first principle] would be this being or that. And if, to such a doubter, a demonstration would

either verify or destroy some one alternative ... this would not destroy his first certain notion of it as a being ... And this proves ... that this certain concept [of God as a being], which of itself is neither of the doubtful ones, is preserved in both of them. (*Ord.* I, d. 3, q. 2, n. 29, *Duns Scotus, Metaphysician,* 111)

One may conceive God as existent, without knowing whether God's being is infinite or finite, and attributing either finitude or infinitude to God does not alter the original concept of being (cf., *Ord.* I, d. 8, q. 4, n. 17). Nonetheless, transcendental being does not refer to anything as such. All beings are either finite or infinite, creatures or the one God. Thus to mark a transcendental concept as uniquely significative of God, we join it with the notion of infinitude. The resultant concept is confused since our finite minds do not comprehend infinitude and hence can never form a perfectly correct picture of the manner in which God's perfections and attributes inhere in his essence, yet the information contained in the transcendental that was united with infinitude provides positive knowledge of God's essence (*Ord.* I, d. 3, pars 1, q. 2, n. 40). These confused yet informative concepts secure the veracity of theological discourse while respecting God's transcendence.

Scotus's theory of transcendental signification relies on a concept of being univocal to God and creatures, for being furnishes the common ground whereby the transcendentals are predicable of both (transcendentals themselves being nothing other than notions that characterize being qua being). Yet if the only distinction between divine and creaturely existence is that the former is infinite, this risks turning being into a genus over and above God and the categories, which Aristotle had shown to be impossible:

It is not possible that ... being should be a genus of things; for the differentiae of any genus must each of them ... have being ... But it is not possible for the genus to be predicated of the differentiae taken apart from the species (any more than for the species of the genus to be predicated of the proper differentiae of the genus); so that if ... being is a genus, no differentia will ... have being. (*Met* III 3, 998^{b}21–26)

Whether or not one is, like Scotus, more or less a realist about the accidents of being, it was in his day traditionally accepted that being is at least derivatively predicable of anything in the ten categories. Specific differences fall within the categories of being, and hence are themselves termed 'beings.' However, if being is itself a genus, then the specific differences would have to be joined with being in order to be termed 'beings,' and this would mean that on their own they had no being, which is impossible insofar as they belong to the categories of being. Still, even if Scotus can render being univocal to God and creatures without making it into a genus, his insistence that being is common to the two suggests either some composition within God (in the form of an element other than his being that makes his being differ from that possessed by creatures), or that the difference between God and creatures is merely one of degree (between infinite and finite being), such that the two are commensurable with respect to being. Neither consequence is acceptable, for both threaten God's transcendence. Let us begin to address these difficulties by looking at some of Scotus's arguments for the existence of concepts univocal to God and creatures.

Scotus understands a concept to be univocal when it 'suffices as a syllogistic middle' capable of linking the major and minor terms of a demonstration (*Ord.* I, d. 3, n. 26, *Duns Scotus, Metaphysician*, 108), and claims to have ten arguments proving that there are concepts univocal to God and creatures.[5] We have already looked at the first of these (recognized by his followers as the strongest),[6] which argues that we can have a concept of God's being without having determined whether that being is finite or infinite. This concept is therefore transcendental, meaning that it subsumes both God and creatures inasmuch as they are beings. Scotus's second argument is that in this life all our concepts are ultimately derived from experience. Thus, if God's being were only characterizable through a concept of being completely alien to our experience 'it would be simply impossible to have any natural concept of God whatsoever. But this is false' (*Ord.* I, d. 3, q. 1, n. 35, *Philosophical Writings*, 22). As a consequence, we can know of God's being through an understanding of being drawn from creatures, but this concept would then be a concept of being univocal to God and creatures (setting aside considerations of finitude and infinitude).

Being is univocally predicable of God and creatures. Consequently concepts of what pertains to being qua being refer univocally to both. Yet, the fact that being is univocal to both seems to make being into a highest genus over and above the two. Furthermore, this univocity threatens God's transcendence. To illustrate the latter point, let us turn to the notions of difference and diversity. Following Aristotle, the scholastics recognize a distinction between what is different (διαφορά) and what is diverse (ἕτερον) (in Latin '*differens*' and '*diversum*,' respectively). Aristotle notes that:

> Everything is either the same as or diverse from[7] everything else … But difference is not the same as diversity. For the diverse and that from which it is diverse need not be diverse in some definite respect (for everything that exists is either diverse or the same), but that which is different from anything is different in some respect. (*Met* X 3, 1054^{b}13–32)

Diverse things need not share anything in common, while things that differ share in one element while differing with respect to another. For example, the ten highest genera are traditionally thought to be diverse from one another, while dissimilar species under the same genus are said to differ by means of their specific differences.[8] God and creatures are also thought to be diverse.

Yet even if Scotus insists that being is not a genus over and above God and creatures, he nonetheless accepts that it is common to both, and this common element threatens to reduce the dissimilarity between them to a mere difference. Scotus is aware of this objection and phrases it as follows:

> How is it possible a concept common to God and creatures be accepted as real save through some reality of its genus [i.e., save through the existence of a genus that subsumes both God and creatures]? And then it seems that there would be potential toward that reality [viz., the specific difference] from which the distinguishing concept is taken … If there were some

reality really distinguishing [them], and distinct from the others [viz., the aforementioned specific difference], it seems that the thing [viz., the entity characterized in terms of genus and specific difference] would be composite, because it would have something with which it agrees [viz., the genus] and something with which it differs [viz., the specific difference. (*Ord.* I, d. 8, pars 1, q. 3, n. 137, trans. mine)[9]

To account for the distinction between creator and creation without reifying being or rendering God's essence composite, Scotus draws on the modal distinction. Unlike the real distinction, which implies composition such that things really distinct from one another are at least theoretically capable of independent existence, the modal distinction does not imply composition. Rather, it is a lesser distinction that acknowledges degrees of intensity within one and the same nature. Scotus discusses this distinction in terms of the color white in the tenth degree:

When some reality [e.g., a color] is understood along with its intrinsic mode [viz., its degree of intensity], that concept is not so absolutely simple that it is impossible that this reality be conceived apart from this mode, although it is then an imperfect concept of the thing. For example: if there were whiteness in the tenth degree of intensity, however simple it may be in reality, it is nonetheless possible that it be conceived under the concept of so much whiteness, and then it would be conceived perfectly by means of a concept adequate to the thing itself. Or, it is able to be conceived precisely under the concept of whiteness, and then it is conceived by means of a concept that is imperfect and lacking in the perfection of the thing. But, the imperfect concept could be in common to this and that white, and the perfect concept is more proper.

Therefore a distinction is needed between that from which a common concept and that from which a proper concept is taken, not in the form of a distinction between one reality and another, but of a reality in its proper and intrinsic modes—which distinction suffices for having a perfect or an imperfect concept of the same thing (of these concepts the imperfect is common and the perfect is more proper)—But the concepts of genus and difference [by contrast] require a real distinction, not merely of the same reality perfectly and imperfectly conceived. (Ibid., nn. 138–39, trans. mine)[10]

Accidents are characterized as inherent in substances; hence, though Scotus allows for a real distinction between most accidents and their subjects (denying, however, that being's proper attributes and the ultimate differentiae are themselves theoretically capable of existing on their own),[11] he nonetheless allows that substance has a priority of being over and above accidents. This is why he terms accidents such as whiteness 'realities (*realitas*)' rather than 'things (*res*).'

Now, we can distinguish between a reality and its mode. Whiteness is distinguishable from the whiteness of an individual, which admits of degree. This is not a real distinction because a quality and its degree do not exist in isolation from one another, unlike various genera and specific differences (such as animality and rationality) which can and are thus really distinct. Accordingly, since the difference between finite and infinite being is merely one of degree between various modes of what has no existence apart from these modes, this difference does not imply any real distinction, and being is not a genus over and above God and creatures. Moreover, the conjunction of a reality and its mode does not entail real composition as the two are not really distinct. Yet, as noted, to conceive of the difference between God and creatures in terms of degree threatens God's transcendence. Chapter 7 discusses Scotus's resolution of this difficulty in light of his conception of God's infinite being.

*

Scotus's belief that being is univocally predicable of God and creatures allows him to assert that whatever pertains to being qua being accurately refers to both. Yet, being qua being does not exist save as an abstract concept (or reality), and the same applies to the perfections and attributes of being qua being. It is not until being and its attributes and perfections are joined with the notion of either infinitude or finitude that they refer uniquely to God or creatures, respectively. Still, the uniquely referring transcendentals are built around a univocal core and our knowledge of this core signification tells us something of the divine essence. However, it is unclear how these attributes inhere in God's infinite and simple essence and whether Scotus allows that their manner of inherence in any way undermines the accuracy of our knowledge of God. Chapter 7 explores Scotus's discussion of God's infinitude in his *Quaestiones Quodlibetales* and *De primo principio* in an attempt to clarify what, if any, impact Scotus believes that God's infinitude has on our ability accurately to conceive his nature.

Chapter 7

Infinitude, Transcendental Signification and Analogy

Scotus believes that transcendental terms signify ideas of attributes and perfections of being that are univocal to God and creatures (*Ord.* I, d. 3, pars 1, q. 2, n. 26). Yet, his decision to refer to these terms as 'univocal' is somewhat misleading. A transcendental concept does not signify any really existent thing until it is joined with the concept of either infinitude or finitude (ibid., d. 8, q. 3, n. 113), and though the meaning of a transcendental term is preserved in this union (ibid., q. 4, n. 17),[1] our finite minds cannot grasp God's infinite being (ibid., d. 22, q. un., Appendix A, 388). This is why our knowledge of the divine essence is confused (ibid., 391). Infinitude thus serves a regulative function in transcendental signification, uniquely determining the reference of concepts attributed to the divine nature, as God is the only infinite entity (*De primo princ.* 4.87–93). Yet our understanding of infinitude does more than determine the reference of transcendental concepts, for reflection on infinite being leads Scotus to draw several conclusions about God's essence. From God's infinitude, Scotus deduces God's simplicity (ibid., 4.75) and unity in diversity (ibid., 4.80), and Scotus's understanding of this unity in diversity impacts his conception of how transcendentals inhere in the divine essence, with which they must be identical owing to God's simplicity. Chapters 5 and 6 examined Scotus's conception of our natural knowledge of God and how this influences his theory of transcendental signification. This chapter discusses Scotus's understanding of infinitude and the mediated quality of our knowledge of God's essence.

*

Owing to his conception of God's infinite being Scotus views our knowledge of the divine essence as incomplete, and only transcendental signification prescinding from consideration of degree can represent God's essence. Scotus's circumspection is likely motivated in part by the unity in diversity that he sees as a concomitant of infinite being. Scotus believes an infinite entity must possess every perfection of being (*Quodl.* 5.8–9) while remaining utterly simple (*De primo princ.* 4.75), though not so simple as to rule out a lesser formal distinction between its attributes.[2] Since God's perfections and attributes are identical with his essence, the transcendental concepts we refer to God are imperfect abstractions, artificially isolating aspects of his nature and thus reflecting the mediated quality of knowledge of God that is drawn from creatures. This may be why Scotus claims that our knowledge of God is confused, it is not inaccurate so much as delimited or incomplete. We know God possesses certain attributes and perfections just as we know that we are unable accurately to conceive how these traits inhere in an essence with which they are identical. Presumably Scotus's claim that transcendentals need to be joined with the notion of infinitude before we may refer them to God is intended to highlight the status of transcendentals as abstract or imperfect representations of God's nature, much as Aquinas's claim that theological discourse must account for God's supereminence is meant to strike a balance between the competing demands of natural knowledge of God and divine simplicity (SCG I.30.3).

*

As white light entering a prism separates into a multitude of colors, God's presence in creation is mediated through creatures and thus experienced in a variety of ways, none of which do justice to the source. Thus God is named 'good' in a manner akin to how white light is named 'red.' White light refracted through a prism may be properly denominable as 'red,' yet white light and red light are not identical in definition. So too God and creatures are conceived through transcendental concepts that present a necessarily inaccurate picture of the divine essence, in which the various perfections of being are present as formally distinct aspects of an utterly simple whole.[3] Scotus's *Quaestiones quodlibetales* elaborates on the mediated character of our knowledge of God's essence.

The fourteenth Question considers whether 'the soul, left to its natural perfection, can know the trinity of persons in God' (*Quodl.* 14.2). First Scotus argues that 'the soul by its natural perfection, considering its nature in any state, is unable to attain knowledge of God that is immediate and proper' (ibid., n. 36), for only God could produce his proper image and he does not will to do this (ibid., n. 37). Then Scotus takes up the question as to whether we might attain mediated knowledge of the trinity:

> I affirm that by their natural powers neither the angel nor the soul in any of its states can have mediate knowledge of the divine essence in all its proper meaning, so that the sense or meaning of that essence would be grasped in knowing or by knowing some intermediary object. (Ibid., n. 74)

Scotus opens this discussion by noting that the difference in degree of being that holds between God and creatures ensures that no creature is capable of serving as a medium that perfectly transmits the divine essence: 'Nothing distinct from divinity contains it perfectly under the aspect of entity; neither then does it contain divinity perfectly under the aspect of knowability' (ibid.). Scotus notes that there are two senses in which something can act as a medium of knowledge, as a medium may be either known or unknown. When we know the medium itself then this medium allows us to know another when knowledge of the medium contains knowledge of the other, 'as is the case when a conclusion is known by means of a principle' (ibid., n. 88). However, a medium cannot furnish knowledge of an object unless 'the knowable object is represented there either properly (i.e., formally) or else virtually' (ibid., n. 78). Scotus denies that anything can contain the divine essence in either manner (ibid., n. 74), and 'if the object exceeds the medium in knowability, then no matter how perfectly the medium is known it will lack something of the knowability of that object' (ibid., n. 88). Thus no medium is known so that by knowing it we completely grasp God's essence.

On the other hand, sometimes the medium itself is unknown but nonetheless conveys knowledge 'in the way, for instance, that the sensible species in the sense faculty is a means of knowing' (ibid.). Sensible species are composed of data that our senses gather about extramental objects. The senses and intellect process and organize these data and produce the phantasms that are the ideas through which extramental objects are present to our intellects.[4] The sensible species themselves provide us with an awareness of extramental objects but we do not conceive these species, thus sensible species are unperceived mediums of cognition. Scotus illustrates the role of the sensible species as an unknown medium with an example of light passing through red glass, which acts as the unperceived medium:

> When a ray of light passes through a piece of red glass, it causes red to appear on the opposite wall. Now the red on the wall is not a means for seeing the red of the glass properly, but one sees the red of the glass only in a derivative sense or perhaps not at all, for there is only some similarity between the red on the wall and that of the glass. But when a sensible species is the reason for perceiving an object properly, then that species itself is not seen by the senses, as is clear in the case of direct vision where nothing intervenes between the color and the eye and still the color is transmitted through the intervening space. (ibid., n. 88)

Scotus has denied that we are able to attain immediate knowledge of the trinity and likewise ruled out our ability perfectly to know the trinity through a known medium. But the same difficulties that prevent our knowing God through a known medium prevent us from knowing him through an unknown medium, for the object must still exceed the medium in knowability. In this case, the possible medium for knowing God would be the soul: 'And what would be the most perfect object that could be represented by it? It would be the soul itself, not God in the fullness of his intelligibility, God could only be dimly mirrored' (ibid., n. 89).

Scotus has considered every possible avenue by which we could arrive at a perfectly proper concept of the divine essence, defined as an intellection *per se*, proper, and immediate, requiring 'the presence of the object in all its proper intelligibility as object' (ibid., n. 36), and in each case ruled against our ability to attain this knowledge. This does not mean that we do not possess knowledge of God; Scotus clearly believes that we do (*Ord.* I, d. 3, pars 1, q. 2, n. 40). Instead, as mentioned, Scotus seems to think that our knowledge is necessarily abstract because this knowledge conceives divine perfections and attributes in isolation from one another, which is how these perfections and attributes manifest in creatures. Scotus discusses the nature of our knowledge of God near the beginning of the Question. In a passage that brings to mind *Ord.* I, d. 22, q. un., he writes:

> What I am saying is that any transcendent notion arrived at by abstraction from what is known of a creature can be thought of in its indifference [i.e., as common and unspecified] and in such a case God is conceived confusedly as it were, just as in thinking of animal, man is being thought of. But if such a common transcendent concept is thought of as qualified by some more specific perfection such as supreme, first, or infinite, we obtain a concept which is proper to God in the sense that it is characteristic of no other being. (*Quodl.* 14.13)

We are able to conceive creaturely attributes indifferently, prescinding from considerations pertaining to finitude and infinitude, and these concepts are confused notions of God's essence. When we join these concepts with our notion of God's infinitude, they remain confused, presumably because we comprehend neither infinity nor the absolute simplicity that is its concomitant, but we obtain a concept that is proper to God. Scotus notes that this concept is not proper in the sense that it provides a completely accurate picture of God's essence, rather the concept is proper because it refers only to God the sole infinite being (*De primo princ.* 4.87–93). Thus, as noted, our knowledge of God is imperfect. However, we should not overlook the importance of faith in Scotus's account. Shortly after he claims that our concepts of God's essence are confused, Scotus considers the role of faith in informing our discourse:

> Belief in the testimony of others can be so firm as to warrant its being called 'knowing [*scire*].' The more truthful the witness, then, the more we can and ought to believe him. And a community can be trusted even more than an individual. The Catholic Church is a most truthful community, however, for it condemns lying and commends truth in the highest measure. Therefore, its testimony can be believed with the greatest of certitude [*certissime credi potest*], especially where it damns a lie the most, in matters of faith and morals. (*Quodl.* 14.20)

Hence a broadly Aristotelian empiricism coupled with faith works in Scotus's theology to steer his account away from apophaticism, which looms as a danger owing to the distance between God and creatures resulting from God's infinite being.

God's Infinitude and Difference in Kind from Creation

Likely Scotus's last complete work, his *De primo principio* demonstrates God's existence by arguing that only a first efficient cause that is itself most perfect and likewise the ultimate final cause could account for the possibility of the universe's existence. From God's status as origin, end, and most perfect, Scotus proceeds to show that God possesses most of the characteristics that Christians traditionally associate with him. Given special attention is God's infinitude, from the knowledge of this 'most fertile [*valde foecundam*]' attribute Scotus claims he might straightaway have deduced 'many of the conclusions' attained earlier in this work (*De primo princ.* 4.47). Though he does not detail the conclusions he has in mind, the notion of God's infinitude is linked to the conclusion that God is utterly simple (ibid., 4.75), in possession of every perfection (ibid., 4.7–11),[5] and wholly identical with the perfections that he possesses (ibid., 4.80). Moreover, Scotus claims that God is incomprehensible, and the manner in which he phrases this claim suggests that God's infinitude is the reason behind it: 'You are infinite and incomprehensible by what is finite' (ibid., 4.46). Indeed, Scotus's discussions of the limits of our understanding of God's nature often bring in considerations pertaining to divine infinitude, which, we shall see, entails the conjunction of God's simplicity and simultaneous possession of every perfection. When Aquinas considers this unity in diversity, he has occasion to remark on the obstacle it raises against God's intelligibility (ST Ia.4.2, arg. 1), and I have suggested that similar considerations motivate Scotus. The link between God's infinitude and his possession of all perfections is especially clear in Scotus's *Quodlibetal Questions*, which likely predate *De primo principio* by about a year.[6]

Scotus's fifth Quodlibetal Question discusses infinitude with respect to the trinity. Scotus opens the investigation by asking us to consider Aristotle's definition of the infinite as 'that whose quantity is such that no matter how much one removes from it, there is always more for the taking [*Physics* III 6, 207^{a}7–9]' (quoted in *Quodl.* 5.5). The portions that one takes from this infinity are discrete quantities. The infinity that these quantities compose is such that no matter how many of these quantities are taken from it, there are always more left to remove. Thus, this infinity is only potentially existent:

> The infinite in quantity, of which the Philosopher speaks, can have being only potentially, if we take one after another. For this reason, no matter how much is removed, what one takes will still be finite and will represent only a certain part of the infinite potential whole. More of it will always remain for the taking. (*Quodl.* 5.5)

This potential infinity is always imperfect, insofar as it can never be in existence as a whole. As a whole, then, it has 'being in the making or potentially' (ibid.).

Keeping in mind this potential infinity, Scotus asks us to imagine the seemingly impossible, that this infinity should exist:

For our purposes, let us change the notion of the potentially infinite in quantity, if possible, to that of quantitatively infinite in act. For just as it is necessary now that the quantity of the infinite should always grow by receiving one part after another, so we might imagine that all the parts that could be taken were taken at once or that they remained in existence simultaneously. If this could be done we would have in actuality an infinite quantity, because it would be as great in actuality as it was potentially. And all those parts which in infinite succession would be actualized and would have being one after the other would be conceived as actualized all at once. Such an infinite in act would indeed be a whole and in truth a perfect whole, since there would be nothing outside it, and it would be perfect, since it lacks nothing. What is more, nothing in the way of quantity could be added to it, for then it could be exceeded. (Ibid., n. 6)

We are then to conceive of God's perfection by using this notion of the quantitatively infinite in act as a model.

If we think of something among beings that is actually infinite in entity, we must think of it along the lines of the actual infinite quantity we imagined, namely as an infinite being that cannot be exceeded in entity by any other being. It will truly have the character of something whole and perfect. It will indeed be whole or complete. (Ibid., n. 7)

Like the quantitatively infinite in act, which could not be exceeded by any other quantity, what is infinite in being (described as infinite 'in entity [*in entitas*]') cannot be exceeded in being by any other entity. Thus it is in possession of every perfection of being, i.e., infinite 'in perfection or power' (ibid., n. 8). This means that everything that pertains to being belongs to the infinite entity. Thus, God possesses all of the pure perfections of being. Moreover, he does so in a way that does not violate his simplicity:

Although something actually infinite in quantity would be perfect as to quantity, because as a whole it would lack no quantity, nevertheless each part of it would lack the quantity of the other parts. That is to say, an infinite of this sort would not be quantitatively perfect [as a whole] unless each of its parts were not imperfect. An infinite being, however, is perfect in such a way that neither it nor any of its parts is missing anything. (Ibid., n. 7)

An infinity composed of discrete quantities is imperfect insofar as each quantity is separate from the others, and thus lacks the perfection of the whole. This is not the case for the entity that is infinite in being. No part of it lacks any other. Scotus does not clarify the reasoning behind this conclusion, but a parallel passage in *De primo principio* provides support:

If the essence [of the infinite entity] were composed its components would be in themselves either finite or infinite. In the first case, the composite would be finite, in the second a part would not be less than the whole. (4.76)

Were an infinite entity in any way composite, its components would have to be either infinite or finite. The latter entails the finitude of an infinite entity, which is impossible; the former, that each part equals the whole, for a part that is itself infinite would equal an infinite whole.

At this point we may recall that Scotus distinguishes God from creation on the grounds that God is infinite while creatures are finite. Yet the distinction between finitude and infinitude must be one of degree to avoid the reification of being into a genus over and above God and creatures. Hence, Scotus attempts to secure God's transcendence by means of a modal distinction. But as modal distinctions are distinctions of degree, Scotus's move threatens to bring God down to the level of a creature by placing him on a scale that comprises creator and creation; for the difference between the two seems to be one of discrete units of being that, added together, could render a creature the equal of its author.

That Scotus would reject this consequence, however, is evident when we look further at his reflections concerning God's infinitude:

> An infinite being is that which exceeds any finite being whatsoever not in some limited degree but in a measure beyond what is either defined or can be defined. Consider whiteness, for instance. It is exceeded triply by another entity, knowledge, or ten times by the intellective soul, or a hundredfold by the most perfect angel. No matter how high you go among beings, there will always be some finite measure according to which the highest exceeds the lowest. Not that there is any proportion or relative measure, properly speaking, as mathematicians use it, because the angel, being simpler, is not constituted by some lesser entity to which something has been added. It must rather be understood as the relative measure of perfection or power in the way one species is superior to another. In this fashion, by contrast, the infinite exceeds the finite in being beyond any relative measure or proportion that could be assigned. (*Quodl.* 5.9)

Scotus believes that the more perfect an entity is the more being it possesses, but his discussion steers us away from thoughts of totaling up the units of being that an entity possesses in order to determine its ontological worth (whatever this would entail), for he notes that there is no 'proportion or relative measure, properly speaking, as mathematicians use it.' Let us stipulate that an angel has eight units of being and a cup one; this does not mean that an angel is eight times better than a cup. Nonetheless, there is a difference between the two and this difference obtains because the angel has more being. Yet even angels are finite, and thus are limited with respect to the being they can receive. They can only get so good. There is no conceivable limit to the degree of being that God possesses; hence no finite being could approximate God's perfection, and the distance between creator and creation is secure. However, Scotus insists that this distance does not prohibit us from acquiring accurate knowledge of God inasmuch as God is a being and thus characterizable in terms of what pertains to being qua being.[7]

Conclusion

Scotus's claim that we possess concepts univocal to God and creatures can be read as a criticism of Aquinas's reliance on analogy of attribution to secure the meaningfulness of theological discourse; and Scotus's introducing his theory in the context of an attack on analogy only reinforces this reading. Yet Scotus's criticism of analogy is directed primarily at Henry of Ghent, whom Scotus views as advancing a type of analogy that robs us of the ability to attain knowledge of God. Scotus does not seem interested in refuting the viability of analogy of attribution as a means of signifying God, he simply dismisses this species of analogy owing to its reliance on prior and posterior signification, and calls any term with multiple significates equivocal. Yet Scotus never rules out the possibility that the significates of equivocal terms may be related. To the contrary, he believes theological discourse relies on terms whose multiple significates are related through core transcendental concepts. Then, to account for the difference between God and creatures, Scotus stipulates that ideas referred to God be joined with the notion of infinitude, seemingly to remind us of the abstract or incomplete nature of our knowledge of God. Aquinas and Scotus certainly differ as to whether one term can signify in a prior and posterior manner, but both believe God's unity in diversity impedes our ability accurately to know his essence and both of their theories of predication are designed to ensure that though impeded, our knowledge of God's essence is not inaccurate. Hence Aquinas asserts that terms said of God retain their meaning but signify in a mode unbefitting the divine essence, while Scotus insists that these terms preserve their original signification (that part of their meaning drawn from experience prescinding from considerations pertaining to finitude) but must be joined with the notion of infinitude, which likewise forces the theologian to account for God's simplicity. These similarities suggest that both Scotus and Aquinas develop theories of the signification of theological discourse that strike a balance between respecting the difference between creator and creation while honoring the generally Aristotelian bent of their natural theology.

Sources Consulted

Primary Sources

Anselm. *Anselm of Canterbury: The Major Works*. Edited with an introduction by Brian Davies and G. R. Evans. Oxford: Oxford University Press, 1998.

Aquinas, Thomas. *Sancti Thomae de Aquino opera omnia*. Edited by Commissio Leonina. Rome: Polyglot Press, 1882–.

—— *Faith, Reason And Theology: Questions I–IV of his 'Commentary on the "De trinitate" of Boethius.'* Translated with introduction and notes by Armand Maurer. Toronto: Pontifical Institute of Mediaeval Studies, 1987.

—— *Summa contra gentiles*. Translated by Anton C. Pegis, et al. Notre Dame: University of Notre Dame Press, 1975.

—— *'Summa theologiae.'* In *Basic Writings of Saint Thomas Aquinas*. Edited and annotated, with an introduction, by Anton C. Pegis. 2 vols. New York: Random House, 1944.

—— *Thomas Aquinas: The Treatise on the Divine Nature; Summa Theologiae I 1–13*. Translated with commentary by Brian Shanley. Introduction by Robert Pasnau. Cambridge: Hackett Publishing Company, 2006.

—— *Commentary on Aristotle's 'De anima.'* Translated by Kenelm Foster and Silvester Humphries. Introduction by Ralph McInerny. Notre Dame: Dumb Ox Books, 1994.

—— *Commentary on the 'Posterior Analytics' of Aristotle*. Translated by F. R. Larcher. Preface by James A. Weisheipl. New York: Magi Books, 1970.

—— *Commentary on Aristotle's 'Metaphysics.'* Translated with an introduction by John P. Rowan. Preface by Ralph McInerny. Notre Dame: Dumb Ox Books, 1995.

Aristotle. *Aristotle in Twenty-Three Volumes.* Loeb Classical Library. Cambridge, MA: Harvard University Press.

—— *The Basic Works of Aristotle.* Edited and with an introduction by Richard McKeon. New York: Random House, 1941.

—— *The Complete Works of Aristotle: The Revised Oxford Translation.* Edited by J. Barnes. 2 vols. Bollingen Series. Princeton: Princeton University Press, 1984.

—— *Aristotle's 'Prior and Posterior Analytics.'* A revised text with introduction and commentary by W. D. Ross. Oxford: Clarendon Press, 1949.

—— *Aristotle: 'Posterior Analytics.'* Translated with a commentary by Jonathan Barnes. 2nd ed. Oxford: Clarendon Press, 1994.

—— *Analytica posteriora.* Edited by L. Minio-Paluello and B. G. Dod. Aristoteles latinus, edited by L. Minio-Paluello 4, pt. 1–4. Bruges and Paris: Desclée de Brouwer, 1968.

Augustine. *De trinitate.* Edited by William John Mountain. Corpus Christianorum, Series Latina 50–50A. Turnholt: Brepols, 1968.

Euclid. *The Thirteen Books Of Euclid's 'Elements.'* Translated with introduction and commentary by Sir Thomas L. Heath. Vol. 1. New York: Dover Publications, 1956.

Hume, David. *Dialogues Concerning Natural Religion, and The Posthumous Essays.* Edited, with an introduction, by Richard H. Popkin. Cambridge: Hackett Publishing Company, 1988.

Maimonides, Moses. *The Guide of the Perplexed.* An abridged edition with introduction and commentary by Julius Guttmann. Translated from the Arabic by Chaim Rabin. New introduction by Daniel H. Frank. Indianapolis: Hackett Publishing Company, 1995.

Plato. *The Collected Dialogues of Plato, Including The Letters.* Edited with introduction and prefatory notes by Edith Hamilton and Huntington Cairns. Princeton: Princeton University Press, 1961.

Porphyry. *Isagoge.* Translated with an introduction and notes by Edward W. Warren. Toronto: Pontifical Institute of Mediaeval Studies, 1975.

Scotus, John Duns. *Opera omnia*. Edited by C. Balić, et al. Vatican Scotistic Commission. Rome: Polyglot Press, 1950–.

—— *Duns Scotus, Metaphysician*. Translated and edited with commentary by William A. Frank and Allan B. Wolter. West Lafayette, IN: Purdue University Press, 1995.

—— *John Duns Scotus, Philosophical Writings: A Selection*. Translated with introduction and notes by Allan Wolter. Foreword by Marilyn McCord Adams. Indianapolis: Hackett, 1987.

—— *John Duns Scotus, God and Creatures: The Quodlibetal Questions*. Translated with introduction, notes, and glossary by Felix Alluntis and Allan B. Wolter. Princeton, Princeton University Press, 1975.

—— *John Duns Scotus, A Treatise on God as First Principle*. Translated and edited with commentary by Allan B. Wolter. Chicago: Franciscan Herald, 1984.

—— *Duns Scotus' 'Questions on the "Categories" of Aristotle.'* Translated and edited by Lloyd Newton. PhD diss., University of Dallas, 2003.

Secondary Sources

Ashworth, E. J. 'Signification and Modes of Signifying in Thirteenth-Century Logic: A Preface to Aquinas on Analogy.' *Medieval Philosophy & Theology* 1 (1991): 39–67.

—— 'Analogy and Equivocation in Thirteenth-Century Logic: Aquinas in Context.' *Mediaeval Studies* 54 (1992): 94–135.

—— 'Analogical Concepts: The Fourteenth-Century Background to Cajetan.' *Dialogue* 31, no. 3 (1992): 399–413.

—— Review of *Aquinas and Analogy*, by Ralph McInerny. *Speculum* (1999): 215–17.

—— 'Medieval Theories of Analogy.' *The Stanford Encyclopedia of Philosophy*. http://plato.stanford.edu/entries/analogy-medieval/, 1999.

Bäck, Allan T. *Aristotle's Theory of Predication*. Philosophia antiqua: A series of Studies on Ancient Philosophy, 84, edited by J. Mansfeld, D. T. Runia, J. C. M. Van Winden. Leiden: Brill, 2000.

Barnes, Jonathan. 'Aristotle, Menaechmus, and Circular Proof.' *The Classical Quarterly*, n.s., 26 (1976): 278–92.

———, ed. *The Cambridge Companion to Aristotle*. Cambridge: Cambridge University Press, 1995.

Bonansea, Bernardino M. 'The Human Mind and the Knowledge of God: Reflections on a Scholastic Controversy.' *Franciscan Studies* 40 (1980): 5–17.

Braswell, Bruce. 'The Use of William of Moerbeke's Recension of the *Posterior Analytics*: A Second Instance.' *Mediaeval Studies* 24 (1962): 371–75.

Broadie, Alexander. *Introduction to Medieval Logic*. 2nd ed. Oxford: Clarendon Press, 1993.

Brown, Stephen, and Stephen Dumont. 'Univocity of the Concept of Being in the Fourteenth Century: III. An Early Scotist.' *Mediaeval Studies* 51 (1989): 1–36.

Burrell, David. 'Aquinas on Naming God.' *Theological Studies* 24 (1963): 183–212.

——— 'John Duns Scotus: The Univocity of Analogous Terms.' *The Monist* 49 (October 1965): 639–58.

——— *Analogy and Philosophical Language*. London: Yale University Press, 1973.

——— *Knowing the Unknowable God: Ibn-Sina, Maimonides, Aquinas*. Notre Dame: University of Notre Dame Press, 1986.

——— 'Recent Scholarship on Aquinas.' *Modern Theology* 18, no. 1 (2002): 109–18.

Chesterton, G. K. *The Collected Works of G. K. Chesterton*. Edited by George William Rutler. Vol. 2. *St. Francis of Assisi*. San Francisco: Ignatius Press, 1986.

——— *The Collected Works of G. K. Chesterton*. Edited by George William Rutler. Vol. 2. *St. Thomas Aquinas*. San Francisco: Ignatius Press, 1986.

Copleston, Frederick. *Aquinas*. London: Penguin Books, 1955.

——— *A History of Philosophy*. Vol. 2, *Mediaeval Philosophy*, pt. 2, *Albert the Great to Duns Scotus*. Garden City, NY: Image, 1962.

Covington, Michael. *Syntactic Theory in the High Middle Ages: Modistic Models of Sentence Structure*. Cambridge Studies in Linguistics. Cambridge: Cambridge University Press, 1984.

Cross, Richard. 'Where Angels Fear to Tread.' *Antonianum* 76 (2001): 7–41.

Dumont, Stephen D. 'The Univocity of the Concept of Being in the Fourteenth Century: John Duns Scotus and William of Alnwick.' *Mediaeval Studies* 49 (1987): 1–31.

—— 'Transcendental Being: Scotus and Scotists.' *Topoi* 11 (Sept. 1992): 135–48.

Flannery, Kevin. Review of *Aquinas and Analogy*, by Ralph McInerny. *Gregorianum* 79 (1988): 381–84.

Flannigan, Thomas-Marguerite. 'The Use of Analogy in the *Summa Contra Gentiles*.' *The Modern Schoolman* 35 (1957): 21–37.

Gilson, Etienne. *The Christian Philosophy of St. Thomas Aquinas*. Translated by L. K. Shook, with a catalogue of St. Thomas's works by I. T. Eschmann. Notre Dame: University of Notre Dame Press, 1956.

Gracia, George G. 'Preface.' *Topoi* 11 (Sept. 1992): 111–12.

—— 'The Transcendentals in the Middle Ages: An Introduction.' *Topoi* 11 (Sept. 1992): 113–20.

Graham, William. 'Counterpredicability and *Per Se* Accidents.' *Archiv für geschichte der philosophie* 57 (1975): 182–87.

Ingham, Mary Beth. *Scotus for Dunces: An Introduction to the Subtle Doctor*. New York: Franciscan Institute Publications, 2003.

Irwin, T. H. 'Aristotle's Concept of Signification.' In *Language & Logos: Studies in Ancient Greek Philosophy Presented to G. E. L. Owen*, edited by Malcolm Schofield and Martha Craven Nussbaum. Cambridge: Cambridge University Press, 1982.

Hankey, Wayne. 'Radical Orthodoxy's *Poiēsis*: Ideological Historiography and Anti-Modern Polemic.' *American Catholic Philosophical Quarterly* 80, no. 1 (2006): 1–22.

Hyman, Arthur, and James J. Walsh, eds. *Philosophy in the Middle Ages: The Christian, Islamic, and Jewish Traditions*. 2nd ed. Indianapolis: Hackett, 1973.

Jordan, Mark. 'The Names of God and the Being of Names.' In *The Existence and Nature of God*, edited by Alfred J. Freddoso, 161–90. University of Notre Dame Studies in the Philosophy of Religion 3. Notre Dame: University of Notre Dame Press, 1983.

—— *Ordering Wisdom: The Hierarchy of Philosophical Discourses in Aquinas.* Notre Dame: University of Notre Dame Press, 1986.

Kenny, Anthony. *The Five Ways: St. Thomas Aquinas's Proofs of God's Existence.* New York: Schocken Books, 1969.

Kirk, G. S., J. E. Raven, and M. Schofield, eds. *The Presocratic Philosophers: A Critical History with a Selection of Texts.* 2nd ed. Cambridge: Cambridge University Press, 1983.

Klima, Gyula. 'Buridan's Logic and the Ontology of Modes.' In *Medieval Analyses in Language and Cognition.* Edited by Sten Ebbsen and Russell L. Friedman, 473–95. Acts of the Symposium of the Copenhagen School of Medieval Philosophy. Copenhagen, 1999.

—— 'Buridan's Theory of Definitions in his Scientific Practice.' In *The Metaphysics and Natural Philosophy of John Buridan.* Edited by Johannes M. M. H. Thijssen and Jack Zupko, 29–47. Medieval and Early Modern Science. Leiden: Brill, 2001.

Knowles, David. *The Evolution of Medieval Thought.* Edited by D. E. Luscombe and C. N. L. Brooke. 2nd ed. London: Longman, 1988.

Kraut, Richard, ed. *The Cambridge Companion to Plato.* Cambridge: Cambridge University Press, 1992.

Kretzmann, Norman *The Metaphysics of Theism: Aquinas's Natural Theology in 'Summa contra gentiles' I.* Oxford: Clarendon Press, 1997.

Kretzmann, Norman, Anthony Kenny, and Jan Pinborg, eds. *The Cambridge History of Later Medieval Philosophy: From the Rediscovery of Aristotle to the Disintegration of Scholasticism, 1100–1600.* Cambridge: Cambridge University Press, 1982.

Kretzmann, Norman, and Eleonore Stump, eds. *The Cambridge Companion to Aquinas.* Cambridge: Cambridge University Press, 1993.

Marmo, Costantino. 'Ontology and Semantics in the Logic of Duns Scotus.' In *On the Medieval Theory of Signs,* edited by Umberto Eco and Constantino Marmo, 143–93. Foundations of Semiotics 21, edited by Achim Eschbach. Philadelphia: John Benjamins Publishing Company, 1989.

—— 'A Pragmatic Approach to Language in Modism.' In

Sprachtheorien in Spätantike und Mittelalter, 169–83. Edited by Sten Ebbesen. Tübingen: Gunter Narr Verlag, 1995.

Marrone, Steven. 'The Notion of Univocity in Duns Scotus's Early Works.' *Franciscan Studies* 43 (1983): 347–95.

—— 'Henry of Ghent and Duns Scotus on the Knowledge of Being.' *Speculum* 63, no. 1 (1988): 22–57.

McInerny, Ralph. *Aquinas and Analogy*. Washington, D.C.: The Catholic University of America Press, 1996.

Mignucci, Mario. *L'Argomentazione dimonstrativa in Aristotele*. Padua: Antenore, 1975.

Newton, Lloyd. 'Duns Scotus's Account of a *Propter Quid* Science of the Categories.' In *Proceedings of the American Catholic Philosophical Association: Reckoning with the Tradition*, edited by Michael Baur, 145–60. New York: American Catholic Philosophical Association, 2005.

Noone, Timothy. 'Alnwick on the Origin, Nature and Function of the Formal Distinction.' *Franciscan Studies* 53 (1993): 231–61.

—— 'Individuation in Scotus.' *American Catholic Philosophical Quarterly* 69 (1995): 527–42.

—— 'The Franciscans and Epistemology: Reflections on the Roles of Bonaventure and Scotus,' 63–90. *Medieval Masters: Essays in Memory of Msgr. E. A. Synan*. Edited by R. E. Houser. Thomistic Papers 7. Houston: Center for Thomistic Studies, 1999.

O'Neill, Blane, and Allan B. Wolter. *John Duns Scotus: Mary's Architect*. Quincy, IL: Franciscan Press, 1993.

Owens, Joseph. 'Common Nature: A Point of Comparison Between Thomistic and Scotistic Metaphysics.' *Mediaeval Studies* 19 (1957): 1–14.

—— 'Analogy as a Thomistic Approach to Being.' *Mediaeval Studies* 24 (1962): 303–22.

—— 'Aquinas—"Darkness of Ignorance" in the Most Refined Notion of God.' In Robert Shahan and Francis Kovach, eds. *Bonaventure and Aquinas: Enduring Philosophers*. Norman, OK: University of Oklahoma Press, 1978.

Pickstock, Catherine. *After Writing: On the Liturgical Consummation of Philosophy*. Oxford: Blackwell Publishers, 1998.

—— 'Duns Scotus: His Historical and Contemporary Significance.' *Modern Theology* 21, no. 4 (2005): 543–74.

Pini, Giorgio. *Categories and Logic in Duns Scotus: An Interpretation of Aristotle's 'Categories' in the Late Thirteenth Century.* Leiden: Brill, 2002.

Plantinga, Alvin. *Does God Have a Nature?* Milwaukee: Marquette University Press, 1980.

Pojman, Louis P., ed. *Philosophy of Religion: An Anthology.* 4th ed. Belmont, CA: Wadsworth, 2003.

Prentice, Robert. 'Univocity and Analogy According to Scotus's "*Super libros elenchorum Aristotelis*".' *Archives d'histoire doctrinale et littéraire du moyen age* 35 (1968): 39–64.

Ross, James. 'Analogy and the Resolution of Some Cognitivity Problems.' *The Journal of Philosophy* 67 (Oct. 1970): 725–46.

—— *Portraying Analogy.* Cambridge: Cambridge University Press, 1981.

Rowe, William L. 'God and Other Minds.' *Noûs* 3 (Sept. 1969): 259–84.

—— *The Cosmological Argument.* New York: Fordham University Press, 1998.

Ryan, John, and Bernardine Bonansea, eds. *John Duns Scotus: 1265–1965.* Vol. 3. Studies in Philosophy and the History of Philosophy. Washington: The Catholic University of America Press, 1965.

Smith, Jerard. *Natural Theology.* New York: The Macmillan Company, 1951.

Stump, Eleonore. 'Aquinas on the Foundations of Knowledge.' *Canadian Journal of Philosophy* 17 (1991): S125–S158.

Torrell, Jean-Pierre. *Saint Thomas Aquinas.* Vol. 1, *The Person and His Work.* Translated by Robert Royal. Washington, D.C.: The Catholic University of America Press, 1996.

Weisheipl, James A. *Friar Thomas D'Aquino: His Life, Thought, and Work.* New York: Doubleday & Company, 1974.

White, Roger. 'Notes on analogical predication and speaking about God.' In *Philosophical Frontiers of Christian Theology*, edited by Brian Hebblewaite and Stewart Sutherland, 197–226. Cambridge: Cambridge University Press, 1982.

Williams, Thomas, ed. *The Cambridge Companion to Duns Scotus.* Cambridge: Cambridge University Press, 2003.

—— 'The Doctrine of Univocity is True and Salutary.' *Modern Theology* 21, no. 4 (2005): 575–85.

—— Review of *The Cambridge Companion to Duns Scotus,* edited by Thomas Williams. *American Catholic Philosophical Quarterly* 80, no. 1 (2006): 146–50.

Wippel, John F. 'Thomas Aquinas on What Philosophers Can Know about God.' *The American Catholic Philosophical Quarterly* 66 (1992): 279–98.

—— *The Metaphysical Thought of Thomas Aquinas: From Finite Being to Uncreated Being.* Washington D.C.: The Catholic University of America Press, 2000.

Wolter, Allan B. *Transcendentals and their Function in the Metaphysics of Duns Scotus.* New York: St. Bonaventure, 1946.

—— *The Philosophical Theology of John Duns Scotus.* Edited by Marilyn McCord Adams. Ithaca, NY: Cornell University Press, 1990.

—— 'Reflections About Scotus's Early Works.' In *John Duns Scotus: Metaphysics and Ethics,* edited by Ludger Honnefelder, Rega Wood and Mechthild Dreyer, 37–57. Leiden: Brill, 1996.

Zupko, Jack. *John Buridan: Portrait of a Fourteenth-Century Arts Master.* Notre Dame: University of Notre Dame Press, 2003.

—— 'Thomas of Erfurt.' *The Stanford Encyclopedia of Philosophy* (Spring 2003 Edition). Edward N. Zalta (ed.). http://plato. stanford.edu/archives/spr2003/ entries/erfurt/

Notes

1. Natural Theology in the High Middle Ages

1   Not all medieval philosophers were professional theologians, only those who matriculated from the faculty of theology. Some medieval scholars, such as Siger of Brabant (d. 1283) and John Buridan (c.1300–c.1361), never went on to this higher faculty, choosing instead careers in the arts faculty, which was responsible for conferring the degrees of bachelor or master. This is not to say that professional theologians such as Aquinas and Scotus were uninterested in purely philo-sophical issues or that arts masters did not discuss theology. Siger, for instance, is notorious for the role he played in shaping theological developments in the thirteenth century (see below). (See also Jack Zupko, *John Buridan: Portrait of a Fourteenth-Century Arts Master* (Notre Dame: University of Notre Dame Press, 2003), 139–45; Anthony Kenny and Jan Pinborg, 'Medieval Philosophical Literature,' in *The Cambridge History of Later Medieval Philosophy From the Rediscovery of Aristotle to the Disintegration of Scholasticism; 1100–1600* (CHLMP), ed. Norman Kretzmann, et al. (Cambridge: Cambridge University Press, 1982), 9–42; and William Courtenay, 'The University of Paris at the Time of Jean Buridan and Nicole Oresme,' *Vivarium* 42, no. 1 (2004): 3–17.

2   As Mark Jordan notes, Aquinas uses 'philosophers (*philosophi*)' to refer to pagan rather than Christian thinkers: Aquinas 'would have been scandalized … to hear himself—or any

Christian—called a "philosopher," since this term often had a pejorative sense for thirteenth-century Latin authors' ('Theology and Philosophy,' in *The Cambridge Companion to Aquinas*, ed. Norman Kretzmann and Eleonore Stump, 232–51 [Cambridge: Cambridge University Press, 1993], 232.)

3   See Paul Vincent Spade, 'Medieval Philosophy,' *The Stanford Encyclopedia of Philosophy* (Fall 2004 Edition), Edward N. Zalta (ed.), http://plato.stanford.edu/archives/fall2004/entries/medieval-philosophy/

4   *Cratylus* 400b–c.

5   Though as Steven Marrone has shown, Henry's later writings downplay the importance of illumination as concerns our ability to attain certainty ('Henry of Ghent and Duns Scotus on the Knowledge of Being,' *Speculum* 63, no. 1 (1988): 22–57).

6   See Bernard Dod's 'Aristoteles Latinus,' in CHLMP, 45–79; and Frederick Copleston, *A History of Philosophy*, Vol. 2, *From Augustine to Scotus* (Garden City, NY: Image, 1962), 205–11.

7   In 1210 the Provincial Council of Paris banned the teaching of Aristotle's natural philosophy. This ban, along with a University statute that prohibited lecturing on Aristotle's metaphysics, was upheld by Robert de Courçon the Papal Legate in 1215. In 1231, Pope Gregory IX maintained the prohibition while appointing a commission to correct the prohibited books. In 1245, Pope Innocent IV extended the prohibition to the University of Toulouse, and in 1263 Urban IV renewed the prohibition of 1210. Nonetheless, by the mid-thirteenth century all of Aristotle's known writings were lectured on at the University of Paris. See Copleston; Spade; and Ralph McInerny, introduction to *Commentary on Aristotle's 'De Anima,'* by Thomas Aquinas, trans. Kenelm Foster and Silvester Humphries (Notre Dame, IN: Dumb Ox Books, 1994).

8   *De Caelo* 1.3, 270^{a}13, 1.12, 281^{b}18; *Physics* 1.9, 192^{a}28, 8.1, 251^{b}19.

9   *De Anima* 3.5, 430^{a}20–26.

10   Ancient philosophers had, for example, arrived at knowledge

of God's infinitude: 'The sayings of the most ancient philosophers are … a witness to this truth. They all posited an infinite first principle of things, as though compelled by truth itself' (SCG I.43.17).

11 In March of 1255 the arts faculty of the University of Paris officially adopted a syllabus imposing the study of the entire Aristotelian corpus, in effect rendering itself a philosophical faculty. This move encouraged thinkers such as Siger to move away from the theology faculty and develop their own ideas. See C. H. Lohr, 'The Medieval Interpretation of Aristotle,' in CHLMP, 80–98.

12 See William Frank and Allan Wolter, eds., *Duns Scotus, Metaphysician* (West Lafayette, IN: Purdue University Press, 1995), 135–44. As noted, this thesis does not reflect Henry's mature thought. Nonetheless, Scotus took this to be Henry's position (e.g., *Ord.* I, d. 22, q. un.).

13 See, Edward Grant, 'The Effect of the Condemnation of 1277,' in CHLMP, 537–40; Robert Pasnau, 'Cognition,' in *The Cambridge Companion to Duns Scotus*, ed. Thomas Williams (Cambridge: Cambridge University Press, 2003), 300–4; and Frank and Wolter (n. 12), 134–44.

14 See Eileen Serene's 'Demonstrative Science,' in CHLMP, 496–518.

15 The term 'Latin Averroism' first appeared in 1899, in Pierre Mandonnet's *Siger de Brabant et l'Averroïsme latin au XIIIe siècle*. Whether the Latin Averroists were as influenced by Averroes as the phrase suggests is debatable. See James A. Weisheipl, *Friar Thomas D'Aquino: His Life, Thought, and Work* (New York: Doubleday & Company, 1974), 272.

16 See Jan Aertsen, 'Aquinas's Philosophy in its Historical Setting,' in *The Cambridge Companion to Aquinas*, ed. Norman Kretzmann and Elenore Stump, 12–37 (Cambridge: Cambridge University Press, 1993), esp. 24–25; M. De Wulf, 'Siger of Brabant,' Sept. 2003, in *The Catholic Encyclopedia*, ed. Kevin Knight, June 2003, http://www.newadvent.org/cathen/13784a.htm; Lohr (n. 11); and Weisheipl (n. 15), 276.

17 For the complete list, see Weisheipl (n. 15), 276.

18   Zdzisław Kuksewicz, 'Criticisms of Aristotelian Psychology and the Augustinian–Aristotelian Synthesis,' in CHLMP, 623–28.

19   Weisheipl (n. 15), pp. 320–23.

20   For a survey of various opinions as to why Aquinas composed his commentaries on Aristotle, see John F. Wippel, *The Metaphysical Thought of Thomas Aquinas: From Finite to Uncreated Being*, Monographs of the Society for Medieval and Renaissance Philosophy 1 (Washington, D.C: The Catholic University of America Press, 2000), xix, n. 17.

21   In 1325, two years after Aquinas's canonization, the Condemnations were repealed insofar as they touched on his writings (see Jean-Pierre Torrell, *Saint Thomas Aquinas*, Vol. 1, *The Person and His Work*, trans. Robert Royal [Washington, D.C: The Catholic University of America Press, 1996], 298–308).

22   Frank and Wolter (n. 12), 134–83; Pasnau (n. 13).

23   Aquinas objects to the doctrine of illumination on the grounds that it makes certainty impossible without God's direct intervention. Human beings are the highest of the sublunary creatures and Aquinas believes that it would be unfitting (and hence a defect in creation) were God to have deprived human beings of the ability to exercise their intelligence without illumination (ST Ia.79.4c). Scotus, on the other hand, believes that Henry of Ghent's doctrine of illumination fails to secure any knowledge of God (see below).

24   Cf. SCG I.11.6.

25   Though Scotus's skepticism regarding the reliability of knowledge (*scientia*) drawn from experience runs deeper than Aquinas's (Serene (n. 14), 496–518).

26   Kuksewicz (n.18), 623–28.

27   See Pasnau (n.13), 300.

28   See, e.g., David Burrell, 'John Duns Scotus: The Univocity of Analogous Terms,' *The Monist* 49, no. 4 (1965): 639–58; and Catherine Pickstock, 'Duns Scotus: His Historical and Contemporary Significance,' *Modern Theology* 21, no. 4 (2005): 543–74. A notable exception is Allan Wolter, who writes: 'A careful analysis of the positions of Duns Scotus and of St. Thomas in the light of their own statements and without the

benefit of well-meaning commentators indicates a far more fundamental agreement between the two men than the superficial treatment characteristic of the average neo-scholastic textbooks, or even reference works, would lead one to believe. Not that the two doctrines are simply identical. Each of the two had his own approach and his own problems. It is the personal opinion of the author that the doctrine of St. Thomas and that of Duns Scotus are fundamentally compatible' (*The Transcendentals and Their Function in the Metaphysics of Duns Scotus* [St. Bonaventure, NY: The Franciscan Institute, 1946], 31, n. 2). This author agrees with the sentiment expressed in Wolter's comments, though I am unaware of his having addressed this issue elsewhere (and hence why he believes Aquinas and Scotus to be fundamentally compatible) or whether he yet maintains this belief.

29   For an overview of the reception of this comment in the Middle Ages, see Alexander Broadie, *Introduction to Medieval Logic*, 2nd ed. (Oxford: Clarendon Press, 1993), 13–19.

30   See Dominik Perler, 'Duns Scotus's Philosophy of Language,' in *The Cambridge Companion to Duns Scotus* (n. 13), 161–92, esp. 163–71.

31   This discussion is drawn from Constantino Marmo, 'Ontology and Semantics in the Logic of Duns Scotus,' in *On the Medieval Theory of Signs*, edited by Umberto Eco and Constantino Marmo, 143–93, Foundations of Semiotics 21, edited by Achim Eschbach (Philadelphia: John Benjamins Publishing Company, 1989), 160–64.

32   *Quaestiones in I librum Perihermeneias*, q. 2, n. 5.

33   Literally: 'concerning its (*suam*) separation.'

34   '*Significat ... hoc nomen homo naturam humanam in abstractione a singularibus. Unde non potest esse quod significet immediate hominem singularem; unde Platonici posuerunt quod significaret ipsam ideam hominis separatam. Sed quia hoc secundum suam abstractionem non subsistit realiter secundum sententiam Aristotelis, sed est in solo intellectu; ideo necesse fuit Aristoteli dicere quod voces significant intellectus conceptiones immediate et eis mediantibus res.*'

35   Whether Plato ever truly believed in these forms or ideas,

and whether if he did once believe in them he continued
to do so throughout his career is debatable, but for his
exposition of the theory of forms I have described, see *Republic*
504e–518c and 596e–597a, *Phaedo* 100b–102a3, and *Phaedrus*
247c3–247e6. For the dating of these works to Plato's middle-
period (c.365–c.347) see Richard Kraut, 'Chronology,' in *The
Cambridge Companion to Plato*, ed. Richard Kraut (Cambridge:
Cambridge University Press, 1992), xii.

36 '*Dicitur quod res primo significatur, non tamen secundum quod
existit, quia nec sic per se intelligitur, sed secundum quod per se
percipitur ab intellectu*' (*Quaestiones in I librum Perihermeneias*,
q. 2, n. 8, trans. mine).

37 With respect to this aspect of the doctrine of illumination as it
was developed by Henry of Ghent, Steven Marrone notes: 'The
doctrine of divine illumination served to describe the mind's
road to God ... This part of the doctrine could perhaps better
be described as the notion of an innate idea of God, as well
as of certain basic concepts ... that seemed best applicable to
the divinity. In knowing the meaning of these concepts, one
had recourse to ideas God actually implanted on the mind
by means of his radiation upon it. It was this aspect of divine
illumination that guaranteed a natural knowledge of the
divinity' ('Henry of Ghent and Duns Scotus,' 24).

38 Though Scotus insists on God's simplicity (*De primo princ.*
4.47) he believes there is a formal distinction between the
divine perfections. Scotus's formal distinction recognizes that
elements of an entity's nature that are in fact inseparable can
still be considered apart from one another and are thus termed
'formally' distinct. This is opposed to a real distinction, such
that really distinct entities can exist apart from one another.
In the case of the divine perfections, however, Scotus insists
that the formal distinction implies even less composition than
it does when applied to elements united in the nature of
ordinary entities, for in creatures these elements perfect one
another, as rationality perfects animality in human beings, but
in the divine essence this is not the case. On the development
of the formal distinction within Scotus's thought, see Timothy

Noone, 'Alnwick on the Origin, Nature and Function of the Formal Distinction,' *Franciscan Studies* 53 (1993): 231–61. For an overview of the role of the formal distinction for Scotus, see Peter King, 'Scotus on Metaphysics,' in *The Cambridge Companion to Duns Scotus* (n. 13), 15–68. On Scotus's understanding of the formal distinction as it applies to the divine essence, see James Ross and Todd Bates, 'Duns Scotus on Natural Theology,' in *The Cambridge Companion to Duns Scotus* (n. 13), 193–238; and *John Duns Scotus: God and Creatures; The Quodlibetal Questions*, trans. with intro. and glossary by Felix Alluntis and Allan Wolter (Washington, D.C.: The Catholic University of America Press, 1975), 505–09.

39 See, e.g., ST Ia.6.4c: 'Plato held the separate existence of the essences of all things, and that individuals were denominated by them as participating in the separate essences; for instance, that Socrates is called man according to the separate form of man.' Cf., ST Ia.15.1, ad 1.

40 Today scholars know that the Pseudo-Dionysius could not have lived before the latter half of the fifth century and was likely a native of Syria. Yet, doubts as to the veracity of Dionysius's claims to be a disciple of St. Paul do not take hold until the Renaissance, in Lorenzo Valla's (1407–1457) glosses on the New Testament (see Jos. Stiglmayr, 'Dionysius the Pseudo-Areopagite,' Aug. 2003, in *The Catholic Encyclopedia*, ed. Kevin Knight, June 2003, http://www.newadvent.org/cathen/05013a.htm).

41 See Frank and Wolter (n. 12), 149.

42 When he says that God is infinite, Aquinas means that God is infinite with respect to 'spiritual magnitude [*spiritualem magnitudinem*]' (SCG I.43.1), which he defines in terms of power and goodness. We must be careful, however, not to think of spiritual magnitude in terms of discrete elements, for this would violate God's absolute simplicity (see SCG I.43.1).

43 See for example Aquinas's discussion of God's goodness in SCG I.38. See also Brian Shanley, *Thomas Aquinas: The Treatise on the Divine Nature: Summa Theologiae I 1-13*, trans. with commentary by Brian Shanley, intro. by Robert Pasnau, The

Hackett Aquinas (Indianapolis: Hackett Publishing, 2006), 194.

44 Note, however, some names attributed to God suggest material limitations not applicable to his essence as in the proposition that God is a lion (Hosea 5:14). Such ascriptions are not literally applicable to God. Rather, Aquinas states that they are metaphorically attributable: 'Whatever names unqualifiedly designate a perfection without defect are predicated of God and of other things: for example, goodness, wisdom, being, and the like. But when any name expresses such perfections along with a mode that is proper to a creature, it can be said of God only according to likeness and metaphor' (SCG I.30.2). In this passage, Aquinas defines metaphor as occurring when 'what belongs to one thing is transferred to another' (SCG I.30.2). For example, Aquinas suggests that we might call a man a stone because of 'the hardness' of his intellect. Aquinas goes on to note that metaphorical names are used 'for the purpose of designating created things [*ad designandum speciem rei creatae*]' (SCG I.30.2, trans. mine). By contrast, 'names that express such perfections [i.e., perfections of created things] along with the mode of supereminence with which they belong to God are said of God alone. Such names are the "highest good," the "first being," and the like' (SCG I.30.2). For a discussion of what Aquinas understands by 'metaphor (*metaphora*),' and how metaphor differs from analogy see Jennifer Ashworth's 'Analogy and Equivocation in Thirteenth-Century Logic: Aquinas in Context,' *Mediaeval Studies* 54 (1992): 94–135.

45 As Brian Shanley notes, 'While this is a crude way of putting it, it is perhaps helpful to see much of Aquinas's doctrine of divine attributes as a skillful exercise in a theological game of Twenty Questions in which the cumulative effect of the negations is to point the questioner in the direction of God without revealing what God is' (*Thomas Aquinas: The Treatise on the Divine Nature*, 201).

46 Cf., ST Ia.13.1, arg. 1: 'It seems that no name can be given to God. For Dionysius says that, "of him there is neither name, nor can one be found of him" [*De Div. Nom.* I, 5].'

47 John Wippel provides a comprehensive overview of Aquinas's use of analogy to name God in *The Metaphysical Thought of Thomas Aquinas*, Monographs of the Society for Medieval and Renaissance Philosophy 1 (Washington, D.C.: The Catholic University of America Press, 2000), 501–75. In addition, Wippel offers support for the view that by the time Aquinas writes his *Summa Contra Gentiles* he has quietly dropped his earlier analogy of proper proportionality—also sometimes called 'Greek analogy' after its source in Greek mathematics where a relation holding between one pair is elucidated in terms of that holding between another: thus three is to six as seven is to fourteen—in favor of the analogy attribution also termed analogy of one-to-another, where a term properly significative of one entity is used in a derivative sense to signify another that is related to the first (see Wippel, *The Metaphysical Thought of Thomas Aquinas*, and 'Thomas Aquinas on What Philosophers Can Know About God,' *The American Catholic Philosophical Quarterly* 66 (Summer 1972): 279–97, especially 294. For a brief overview of various theories of analogy at play in the Middle Ages see Jennifer E. Ashworth, 'Medieval Theories of Analogy,' *The Stanford Encyclopedia of Philosophy* (Winter 1999 Edition), Edward N. Zalta (ed.), http://plato.stanford.edu/ archives/win1999/ entries/analogy-medieval/

48 On the relation between our concepts and extramental entities, see Jennifer Ashworth, 'Signification and Modes of Signifying in Thirteenth-Century Logic: A Preface to Aquinas on Analogy,' *Medieval Philosophy & Theology* 1 (1991): 39–67; and on the order according to the name and the order according to reality see Ashworth, 'Analogy and Equivocation in Thirteenth-Century Logic,' 94–135, especially 124–26.

49 Etienne Gilson, *The Christian Philosophy of St. Thomas Aquinas*, trans. L. K. Shook (Notre Dame: University of Notre Dame Press, 1956), 106.

50 Ibid., 107.

51 Cf., Maimonides, *Guide* I, 58.

52 Alain of Lille, *Theologicae Regulae* XXI; XXVI. Note though, in

De potentia, q. 7, a. 5, Aquinas attributes this view to Maimonides (see Wippel, *The Metaphysical Thought of Thomas Aquinas*, 2000, 537).

53 Aquinas appears to contradict his assertion that theological discourse signifies God in the manner that 'healthy' signifies medicine and human beings (see above and SCG I.34.5). But we need not suppose that this is the case. In this passage (ST Ia.13.2c) Aquinas asserts that the perfections we ascribe to God belong to his essence; God is not called 'good' merely because he makes creatures good but because he *is* good. Again though in ST Ia.13.5c Aquinas uses the example of medicine termed 'healthy' to illustrate his point that God is known and named through his effects, he modifies his account to indicate that suggests he believes God actually possesses the perfections in question: 'Whatever is said of God and creatures is said according as there is some relation of the creature to God as to its principle and cause, *wherein all the perfections of things pre-exist excellently*' (italics mine). Thus Aquinas's comment in ST Ia.13.2c serves as a warning not to take the medicine–patient understanding of analogy too literally. To call God 'good,' 'wise,' etc., is to say more than that he causes these properties in others.

54 Cf., ST Ia.13.2, ad 2: 'Divine names are imposed from the divine processions; for as according to the diverse processions of their perfections, creatures are the representations of God, although in an imperfect manner, so likewise our intellect knows and names God according to each kind of procession. But nevertheless these names are not imposed to signify the processions themselves, as if when we say God lives, the sense were, life proceeds from Him, but to signify the principle itself of things, in so far as life pre-exists in Him, although it pre-exists in Him in a more eminent way than is understood or signified.'

55 Scotus does not accept the existence of analogy of attribution because he does not believe that one term can signify one concept that refers primarily to one entity and secondarily to another (see below). In addition, he holds that the theory of analogy developed by Henry of Ghent rests on a

logical impossibility, viz., that a term can signify properties pertaining to God's essence without telling us anything of that essence (see below). It is Henry's analogical terms that Scotus describes as meaningless. Scotus's denial of analogy of attribution is influenced by the semantics of the speculative grammarians or *Modistae*—grammarians and logicians whose work was influential in Paris during the latter half of the thirteenth century through the first decade of the fourteenth (see Michael Covington, *Syntactic Theory in the High Middle Ages: Modistic Models of Sentence Structure*, Cambridge Studies in Linguistics (Cambridge: Cambridge University Press, 1984); Jack Zupko, 'Thomas of Erfurt,' *The Stanford Encyclopedia of Philosophy* (Spring 2003 Edition), Edward N. Zalta (ed.), http://plato.stanford.edu/ archives/ spr2003/entries/erfurt/); Constantino Marmo, 'A Pragmatic Approach to Language in Modism,' in *Sprachtheorien in Spätantike und Mittelalter*, ed. Sten Ebbesen, (Tübingen: Gunter Narr, 1995), 169–83; and Ashworth, 'Analogy and Equivocation in Thirteenth-Century Logic'—and as I shall argue, Scotus's denial that one term can signify in a primary and posterior manner does not put him at odds with Aquinas as regards what can be known of the divine essence. That is, their divergent understandings of signification do not reflect different conceptions of our natural knowledge of God so much as Scotus's rejection of the modist interpretation of analogy. In addition, it is unclear whether Aquinas himself believes that in analogy of attribution one term signifies just one idea that refers primarily to one thing and secondarily to another. Sometimes he speaks this way (e.g., *Scriptum super libros Sententiarum* 19.5.2, ad 1), other times he maintains that there are multiple significates (*De principiis naturae* 6), and in his *Summa theologiae* he argues for something in between (ST Ia.13.5c). See Ashworth, 'Analogy and Equivocation in Thirteenth-Century Logic,' 124. My thanks to an anonymous scholar at the 2006 meeting of the International Duns Scotus Society for bringing Aquinas's shift on this issue to my attention.

56 For Scotus's use of this terminology, see Giorgio Pini, *Categories*

and Logic in Duns Scotus: An Interpretation of Aristotle's 'Categories' in the Late Thirteenth-Century (Leiden: Brill, 2002), 173.

57   See Frank and Wolter (n.12), 105, n. 4; and P. Coffey, 'Henry of Ghent,' July 2004, http://www.newadvent.org/cathen/ 0723b. htm.

58   Frank and Wolter (n.12), 136.

59   After Scotus's death, the opinion of Henry was generally incorporated into a broader Thomistic framework, which may have encouraged subsequent thinkers to view Scotus in opposition to Aquinas, despite the insistence of some of Scotus's earliest disciples—Peter of Navarre (d. 1347) and Peter of Aquila (d. 1361)—that Scotus and Aquinas are in fundamental agreement. This is not to say that all of Scotus's disciples held this opinion, as Antonius Andreas's (d. 1320) interpretation of Scotus does put Scotus at odds with Aquinas. See Stephen Dumont, 'Transcendental Being: Scotus and Scotists,' *Topoi* 11, no. 2 (1992): 135–48.

60   Frank and Wolter (n.12), 176, n. 7.

61   It is interesting to note that Scotus relies on this same passage to justify his thesis that we are able to arrive at concepts that are proper or refer uniquely to God: 'From the knowledge of an individual being, the meaning of "being" itself can be known by abstraction. The same is true of "good." And this takes place in the way Augustine indicates when he writes: "Consider this good and that good. Take away the *this* and the *that* and view *good* itself, if you can, and then you will see God." And in the same passage he [viz., Augustine] goes on to show how God can be known not only in this quasi-confused concept of good, but also in a concept that is in some sense proper to him, for example, if one thinks of the highest good or of what is good by its essence' (*Quodl.* 14.12).

62   Scotus does not actually believe that physical beings are in a continual state of flux. He is granting this premise for the sake of argument: 'It is also clear that the antecedent of this argument is false, viz., that what the senses can perceive is continually changing' (*Ord.* I, d. 3, pars. 1, q. 4, n. 218, *Philosophical Writings*, 103).

63 See Timothy Noone, 'The Franciscans and Epistemology: Reflections on the Roles of Bonaventure and Scotus,' in *Medieval Masters: Essays in Memory of Msgr. E. A. Synan*, ed. R. E. Houser (Houston, TX: Center for Thomistic Studies, 1999), 63–90.

64 '*Negat conceptum communem univocum Deo et creaturae et ponit duos conceptus analogos (quorum scilicet alter, qui est creaturae, attribuitur alteri, scilicet illi qui est Dei).*' Cf. *Ord.* I, d. 3, pars 1, q. 1, nn. 20–21. For Henry's statement of his position see his *Summa* 21.2, ad 3.

65 *Philosophical Writings*, 38, n. 6.

66 See also King, 'Scotus on Metaphysics' (n. 38), 26.

67 Marmo, 'A Pragmatic Approach to Language in Modism' (n. 55), 170.

68 See Ross and Bates, 'Duns Scotus on Natural Theology' (n. 38) 193–237, esp. 213; and *Ord.* I, d. 8, q. 4, n. 17.

69 Scotus echoes this sentiment elsewhere, e.g: 'We neither have, nor can have ... a comprehensive act of knowledge in regard to an infinite object' (*Ord.* I, d. 3, q. 3, *Philosophical Writings*, 32). This is important to note in light of Catherine Pickstock's comment that by Scotus's 'concept of a positive infinite, one "grasps" an absolute void of mystery,' which she follows by noting that for Scotus this infinity is 'comprehended' ('Duns Scotus: His Historical and Contemporary Significance,' *Modern Theology* 21 (2005), 543–74, at 563). Pickstock also suggests that Scotus's conception of divine infinitude as something we can grasp violates the gap between creator and creation: 'Does not this approach in some slight way impugn divine omnipotence, and render God a being alongside other beings, even if this "alongside" is a nonnegotiable gulf (and even because it is a nonnegotiable gulf)?' (ibid., 553–54). In an earlier work, Pickstock claims that, for Scotus, 'God is deemed "to be" in the same univocal manner as creatures ... [but] the univocity of Being between God and creature paradoxically gives rise to a kind of equivocity, for the difference of degree or amount of Being disallows any specific resemblance between them' (*After Writing: On the Liturgical Consummation of Philosophy* (Oxford:

Blackwell Publishers, 1998), 122–23. The common theme in these works seems to be Pickstock's belief that Scotus renders God like us but places him beyond our understanding 'thus the same becomes radically disparate and unknowable' (ibid., 123), which, in turn, is thought to entail several 'epistemological and theological manoeuvres' (ibid.), including the establishing of 'contractual relations between the creature and God' (ibid.). Yet Scotus's belief that bare transcendentals do not refer and that when joined with infinitude they signify attributes that belong in the divine essence in a way we cannot fathom does not necessitate that God is disparate and unknowable so much as that he possesses and is identical with every perfection. How is Scotus any more likely to cut us off from God than Aquinas, whom Pickstock characterizes as introducing 'us to a mysterious and yet palpable darkness, which in refusing our analysis, still welcomes us' ('Duns Scotus,' 563–64)? Pickstock links her assertion to Scotus's allowance for a positive concept of infinity (ibid.), but as we have seen, Scotus believes that this is an infinity that we cannot comprehend.

2. Aquinas and *Scientia*

1   Throughout, my discussion of *scientia* has benefited from W. D. Ross's, *Aristotle's 'Prior and Posterior Analytics,'* rev. with intro. and commentary by W. D. Ross (Oxford: Clarendon, 1949). Ross's commentary on Aristotle's aporia may be found on pp. 506–07.

2   Allowing for this definition of thunder, one can imagine that the extinction of water in a cloud might for some reason occasionally fail to produce noise. Nonetheless, because of the type of event it is, thunder will produce noise when the proper conditions are met. Thus the property is still essential to thunder in the sense that the property is necessarily connected with the nature of the event.

3   See, Ross (n.1) 637–47; and *Aristotle: 'Posterior Analytics,'* ed. and trans. Hugh Tredennick, Vol. 2 *Aristotle,* The Loeb Classical

Library (Cambridge, MA: Harvard University Press, 1960), 208–09, n. *e*.

4   Aquinas dismisses the relevance to *scientia* of the third type of *per se* belonging—described by Aristotle as 'what is not said of some underlying subject' (*An.Post* I 4, 73^{b}5–6)—on the grounds that 'this mode is not a mode of predicating, but a mode of existing' (In PA I.10).

5   Unless otherwise indicated, translations from the Latin *An.Post* are Larcher's and translations from the Greek *An.Post* are Barnes's.

6   Note, rather than '*subiectis* (subjects)' the Greek only has forms of the intensive pronoun 'αὐτό' meaning simply 'self,' and reads 'One thing belongs to another in itself ... if the things it belongs to themselves belong in the account which makes clear what it is' (trans. Barnes).

7   For the Greek of the *Posterior Analytics*, I use Ross's critical edition, which is compiled from the five oldest Greek manuscripts (Urbinas 35 (A) (9th–early 10th c.), Marcianus 201 (B) (955), Coislinianus 330 (C) (11th c.), Laurentianus 72.5 (d) (11th c.), and Ambrosianus 400 (olim L 93) (n) (9th c.)). For the Latin, I rely on the 1989 Leonine edition, and Minio-Paluello and Dod's critical editions of the thirteenth century's three Greek to Latin translations (L. Minio-Paluello and B. G. Dod, eds., *Analytica posteriora, Aristoteles latinus* (AL), 4, pt. 1–4 [Bruges and Paris: Desclée de Brouwer, 1968]). The first and most widely read translation was produced sometime in the second quarter of the twelfth century by James of Venice (*Iacobus Venetici*), of whom little is known (Minio-Paluello, preface, II.1; and Bernard Dod, '*Aristoteles Latinus*,' in CHLMP, 45–79, esp. 54–55). The second translation came out sometime before 1159, when it is cited in John of Salisbury's *Metalogicon*, and is likely a *recensio* of James's. Less still is known of its translator, whose name may have been John (*Ioannes*) (Minio-Paluello, preface, III; Dod, 56–57). Finally, there is the translation of William of Moerbeke (*Guillelmum de Moerbeka*), which was produced around 1269, and adopted by Aquinas around 1271 (Jean-Pierre Torrell, *Saint Thomas Aquinas*, Vol. 1, *The Person and*

His Work, trans. Robert Royal [Washington, D.C.: The Catholic University of America Press, 1996], 226–27). Before getting hold of Moerbeke's translation, Aquinas worked with James's. Specifically, Aquinas comments on James's translation through to I 27 and then switches to Moerbeke's (ibid.). Comparing these translations with surviving editions of the Greek, Minio-Paluello concludes that at I 4 James's text is nearest to the Marcianus edition, while both John's and Moerbeke's Greek editions bear a close resemblance to the Coislinianus manuscript (for James, John and Moerbeke, respectively, see Minio-Paluello, preface, XLIII, LI, and LXXXII).

8   Ordinarily, one would take '*in simpliciter scibilibus*' with '*dicuntur*,' producing 'those things that are said to be absolutely scientifically knowable.' However, in the Greek '*ἐπὶ τῶν ἁπλῶς ἐπιστητῶν* [in the case of what is absolutely scientifically knowable]' is parenthetical information that separates '*τὰ ... λεγόμενα* [the things called]' from '*καθ᾽ αὐτὰ* [*per se*]'. This practice of retaining Greek word order at the expense of Latin grammar was common among medieval translators of Aristotle. For a discussion of this practice, see '*Aristoteles Latinus*' (n. 7), 64–70.

9   See Ross (n. 1) 522.

10 Ross (n. 1), 522, and Tredennick (n. 3), 47.

11 Note in the second edition of his commentary on the *Posterior Analytics*, Barnes opts instead for 'subjects': 'The phraseology has caused difficulty. The solution (see Mignucci (1975), 75–6) is that Aristotle here uses *τοῖς κατηγορουμένοις* ("what is predicated") to refer to the *subject* terms of the propositions. The verb *κατηγορεῖν* sometimes means "to apply a predicate to" ... so that *τὰ κατηγορουμένα* are the items to which predicates are applied' (Aristotle, *Posterior Analytics*, trans. with a commentary by Jonathan Barnes, 2nd ed. (Oxford: Clarendon Press, 1994), 117.

12 Ross (n. 1), 522, and Tredennick (n. 3), 44, n. *d*.

13 Ibid., 44, n. *d*.

14 The quote from Aristotle is my own translation from the Latin. The rest of the passage is translated by Larcher.

15 For a discussion of counterpredication, see Robin Smith, 'Logic,' in Jonathan Barnes, ed., *The Cambridge Companion to Aristotle*, 27–63 (Cambridge: Cambridge University Press, 1995), 54.

16 The distinction between proper accidents and definitions, both of which are counterpredicable but only one of which, viz., definitions, captures the essential nature of a thing, is somewhat unclear. In the introduction to his translation of Porphyry's *Isagoge*, Edward Warren notes the difficulty inherent in distinguishing proper accidents from the differences that go into a thing's defining formula and suggests that: 'the answer lies in the notion that an accident is not connected to the essence as a natural tendency, and, therefore, is predicated *primarily* to the degree that it actually exists in a singular. The difference, however, is predicated in terms of the essence as fulfilled in the attainment of the end, τὸ τέλος or τὸ τί ἦν εἶναι' (*Isagoge*, 58, n. 52). For instance, the ability to laugh as predicated of Cicero and Cato differs 'to the extent that they tend to laugh' (Boethius, *Editionis Secundae Commenta Boethii*, 309, 2–5; quoted in Porphyry, *Isagoge*, trans. with intro. and notes by Edward W. Warren [Toronto: The Pontifical Institute of Mediaeval Studies, 1975], 58, n. 52). In other words, proper accidents are dispositions whose realization is partially dependent on the character of the individuals who possess them. Nevertheless, knowledge of proper accidents would remain productive of *scientia* as *scientia* of universal (though unequally actualized) potentiality.

17 Ross, however, notes that there is no reason to limit such attributes to pairs, explaining that a triangle, for instance, can be equilateral, scalene, or isosceles; but he seems to accept that attributes that belong *per se* in the second manner are mutually exclusive (see Ross (n. 1), 519).

18 In *The Five Ways: St Thomas Aquinas' Proofs of God's Existence* (New York: Schocken Books, 1969), Anthony Kenny notes that over the course of his career, Aquinas recognized two distinct senses of necessity. At first he adapted a Leibnizian sense of necessity inspired by Avicenna, where a necessary

being is one the supposition of whose non-existence entails a contradiction. By the time of writing the *Summa contra gentiles*, however, Aquinas adopted a sense of necessity drawn from Averroes. In this new sense, necessity is defined 'not in terms of essence and existence, but in terms of unalterability, following Aristotle's definition of the necessary as that which cannot be otherwise (*Metaphysics* V 5, 1015ª34). In this sense, something is necessarily the case if it cannot cease to be the case' (48). It is this latter sense of necessity that is apparently at work in Aquinas's commentary.

19 '*cum causam quoque arbitramur cognoscere propter quam res est, et quoniam illius est causa, et non est contingere aliter se habere.*'

20 Following Aristotle, Aquinas believes that certain traits belong to things owing to their natures, as, e.g., humans are risible owing to their humanity. Thus, borrowing a phrase from Ross, we may term natures or essences 'ontological causes' with respect to the particular entities to which they belong.

21 '*Quia ... scientia est perfecta cognitio, dicit: "cum causam arbitramur cognoscere"; quia vero est actualis cognitio per quam scimus simpliciter, addit: "et quoniam illius est causa"; quia vero est certa cognitio, subdit: "et non est contingere aliter se habere."* '

22 Note there must be one exception to this rule if Aquinas is to demonstrate with scientific certainty that God exists, for as an individual entity, God would not ordinarily be an object of scientific knowledge. The reason that Aquinas can make an exception for demonstrations of God's existence is presumably that God is necessarily existent. Hence, even if God is an individual entity, the claim that he exists is necessarily true. Of course this presumes Aquinas's demonstrations of God's existence are scientific, a claim I defend in Chapter 3.

23 Recall Aquinas's earlier assertion that the conclusion of a scientific demonstration actually asserts *two* modes of *per se* belonging, viz., the second and the fourth (In PA I.10.8 = *An.Post* 73ᵇ16–17). The apparent discrepancy between this earlier passage and the one we are now considering likely emerges from the fact that the fourth mode of *per se* belonging

takes in the first and second. With this understood, Aquinas need not mention the fourth mode every time he discusses the other two.

24 Thomas Heath, ed., *The Thirteen Books of Euclid's 'Elements,'* trans., with intro. and commentary by Thomas Heath, 2nd ed., rev., vol. 1, *Introduction and Books I, II* (New York: Dover Publications, 1956), 120.

25 Ross (n. 1), 602; *An.Post* 72ª17–18.

26 Ross (n. 1), 531; Heath (n. 24), 119.

27 Literally translated: 'There are four things that are asked, namely: that, on account of what, if it is, and what it is [*quatuor autem sunt quae quaeruntur, scilicet quia, propter quid, si est et quid est*]' (In PA II.1.2, trans. mine).

28 Barnes translates Aristotle's '*συμφωνία*' with 'harmony.' I replace 'harmony,' 'harmonize' with 'concordance' and 'concord' to bring Barnes' translation in line with Larcher's.

29 On Aquinas's apparent willingness to extend this schematism to cover both demonstration *propter quid* and demonstration *quia* see In PA I.13.11.

30 In PA II.1.9.

3. *Scientia, Analogia,* and the Five Ways

1 ST Ia.2.2, ad 1. '*Scibile,*' from the verb '*scire,*' 'to know,' can mean simply 'knowable' or 'discernable.' Below, I explain why I believe this passage uses the term in the technical sense of 'scientifically knowable.'

2 See In PA II.1.8, 186–87 = *Posterior Analytics* (*An.Post.*), II 2, 90ª5–11.

3 In Chapter 2 it was noted that there are two types of demonstration that rely on effects to disclose that something is the case with respect to their cause. Demonstration *quia* is one type. The other would be a demonstration *si est*, which concludes simply that the cause of some effect exists: 'The proposition is formed in two ways: in one way from a noun and a verb without any appositive, as when it is stated that *a*

man is; in another way when some third item is set adjacent, as
when it is stated that *a man is white*' (In PA II.1.3). Thus strictly
speaking a demonstration that God exists would be demonstration *si est* (concluding with a verb and a noun without any
appositive) rather than demonstration *quia* (where a third
item is set adjacent).

4   For a discussion of why an infinite regress might be possible,
    see Kenny, *The Five Ways*, 24–27.

5   Note that if this argument succeeds, it shows only that some
    being that is pure actuality must exist. To identify this being
    with God, Aquinas will argue that whatever possesses pure
    actuality must likewise possess the perfections that Christians
    traditionally associate with God. I consider Aquinas's line of
    reasoning below when I discuss his Fourth Way.

6   As noted, nominal definitions do not always pick out traits
    that are essential to their subjects. This raises a difficulty. If
    Aquinas's proofs of God's existence do not show that no being
    save God could produce the phenomena adduced in support
    of God's existence, the Five Ways do not force us to conclude
    that God exists. Put another way, Aquinas has to show that
    God's existence is the necessary condition of the phenomena
    used to demonstrate his existence. Aquinas's discussion in ST
    Ia.3.5c does not explicitly address this difficulty. However, over
    the course of his demonstrations and in reflections that follow,
    he furnishes a way of meeting it. This is because the nominal
    definitions employed in Aquinas's demonstrations are such
    that they could only belong to a being that is pure actuality.
    For instance, the First Way defines God as the 'first mover' (ST
    Ia.2.3c), which, it emerges, entails his being pure actuality (ST
    Ia.3.1c). Being pure actuality, God is immaterial (ST Ia.3.1c).
    The essence of an immaterial being is unique, seeing that this
    essence is not multiplied by matter (ST Ia.3.3c), thus no other
    being could account for the phenomena used to adduce God's
    existence.

7   See *Met* IV 2.

8   See ST Ia.13.1, ad 1; and Brian Shanley's commentary in *The
    Treatise on the Divine Nature: "Summa theologiae" I 1-13*, 326.

9   At least one further stipulation is needed though it does not bear directly on Aquinas's use of analogy of attribution to name God; namely, an entity '*x*' less properly characterizable in terms of *F* than is God may itself be the reason that *F* is said of another entity '*y*' less properly characterizable in terms of *F* than either *x* or God (as individual beings are the reason that accidents themselves may be termed 'beings'). This reflects the use of analogy of attribution outside of theological discourse.

10   '*Nihil tamen prohibet illud quod secundum se demonstrabile est et scibile, ab aliquo accipi ut credibile, qui demonstrationem non capit.*'

11   I discuss these texts in Chapter 2; see also Minio-Paluello and Dod, eds., *Analytica posteriora, Aristoteles latinus* (AL), preface; Dod, '*Aristoteles latinus,*' in CHLMP, 75; and Torrell, *Saint Thomas Aquinas*, Vol. 1, 226–27.

12   The translations are those of James of Venice, Ioannes (likely a *recensio* of James's work), William of Moerbeke, and Gerard of Cremona. The first three are from the Greek, the fourth from the Arabic translation (*Analytica posteriora*, preface).
James: *Demonstrationem autem dico sillogismum … facientem scire* (AL, 7).
Ionnis: *Demonstrationem autem dico sillogismum facientem scire* (AL, 113).
Guillemi: *Demonstrationem autem dico sillogismum scientificum. Scientificum autem dico secundum quem in habendo ipsum scimus* (AL, 286).
Gerardi: *Per demonstrationem vero significo sillogismum compositum veridicum quo scitur res secundum quod ipsa est* (AL, 189).

13   A discussion of the use of the expression '*scientia demonstrativa*' throughout the Middle Ages can be found in Eileen Serene's 'Demonstrative Science,' in *CHLMP*, 496–517. On Aquinas's realization of the natural theologian's need for a demonstration of God's existence, see SCG I.9.5: 'Now, among the inquiries that we must undertake concerning God in himself, we must set down in the beginning that whereby his existence is demonstrated, as the necessary foundation of the whole work. For, if we do not demonstrate that God exists, all consideration of divine things is necessarily suppressed.' Cf., Thomas

Williams (who maintains that Aquinas's demonstrations are scientific in the technical sense): 'The Doctrine of Univocity is True and Salutary,' *Modern Theology* 21, no. 4 (Oct. 2005): 575–85, esp. 580–81. Catherine Pickstock, on the other hand, denies that Aquinas's demonstrations are scientific ('Duns Scotus: His Historical and Contemporary Significance,' *Modern Theology* 21, no. 4 (2005): 543–74, esp. 570, n. 4). This harmonizes with her assertion that Aquinas's *via negativa* 'introduces us to a mysterious and yet palpable darkness, which in refusing our analysis, still welcomes us' (ibid., 564). See Chapter 1 above for my discussion of Pickstock's claim.

14   The phrase is Norman Kretzmann's. For his discussion of the initial disparity between these explanatory beings and the God of revelation see 'The Existence of Alpha,' in *The Metaphysics of Theism: Aquinas's Natural Theology in 'Summa contra gentiles' I* (Oxford: Clarendon Press, 1997), chap. 3.

15   Cf., Shanley, 190: 'God is the First Unmoved Mover. The First Unmoved Mover Exists. Therefore God exists.'

16   For the First Way to be scientific, existence must be a *per se* accident of the first mover. Discussion of what this might mean was put off in order to consider whether Aquinas's demonstration meets the requirements of analogy of attribution. Now we may note that if the first mover is indeed the cause of the existence of all else, Aquinas's comment that existence is the proper effect of the cause of the existence of all else (*esse est eius proprius effectus*) (SCG II.22) allows us to argue that existence is a *per se* accident of the first mover. For, a proper effect is a property, or that which only belongs to one type of thing and yet is not mentioned in the definition of that type (Aristotle, *Topics*, I 5, 102^{a}18–21). Scholars have disputed whether or not properties are to be identified with *per se* accidents (in favor of the identification, see *Aristotle's 'Prior and Posterior Analytics'*, ed. Ross, 60; against it, see Jonathan Barnes, 'Properties in Aristotle's Topics,' *Archiv für Geschichte der Philosophie* 52 (1970): 136–55, esp. 139–40). Aquinas, for his part, seems to accept the identification; for, at least once, he uses the two terms interchangeably (In PA I.35.7, 91–114 = *An.Post.* I 22, 84^{a}22–24). So,

if Aquinas holds that *per se* accidents are identical to properties, to say that existence is a property of the first mover is to say that it is a *per se* accident of the first mover (though the *per se* causality entailed by this claim must be analogically predicated in the manner discussed above).

17 See William Rowe, *The Cosmological Argument* (New York: Fordham University Press, 1998), chap. 1; Kenny (n. 4), 41; and Shanley (n. 4), 192–95.

18 See Kenny (n. 4), 42–43.

19 For this distinction between logical and ontological necessity, see Chapter 2. On the necessity Aquinas has in mind with respect to the Third Way, see Kenny (n. 4), 48; and Rowe (n. 17), 40–41.

20 Though the heavenly bodies must retain potentiality with regard to place.

21 Technically this is a hypothetical necessity, in this example dependent on something's being human. In addition, the power of form is limited by material considerations (see, e.g., ST Ia.92.1, ad 1), a view inherited from Aristotle (see, e.g., *Generation of Animals,* IV 3).

22 See Kenny (n. 4), 48.

23 This proof appears to draw on the so-called Principle of Plenitude, widely held among the medieval schoolmen, which states that 'No genuine possibility can remain forever unrealized.' If this principle holds, were all entities corruptible, eventually they would all cease to exist. Hence necessary entities exist. (For this formulation of the principle as well as a discussion of its Aristotelian origin, see Simo Knuuttila, 'Modal Logic,' in CHLMP, 342–57.) Modern commentators have objected that in a universe full of naught save contingent entities there need never be a time when all entities have ceased to exist (Rowe (n. 17), 42–43; Kenny (n. 4), 56; Shanley (n. 8), 195–96). Following Rowe, where 'Cx' = 'x is a contingent entity,' 'Ty' = 'y is a time' and 'Exy' = 'x exists at y': from '(x) $[Cx \supset (\exists y) (Ty \cdot \sim Exy)]$,' Aquinas infers '$(\exists y) [(Ty \cdot (x) (Cx \supset \sim Exy)]$,' i.e., from 'Each x is such that if x is contingent then there exists a time "y" such that x does not exist at "y,"'

Aquinas infers 'There exists a y such that y is a time and every x is such that if x is contingent then x does not exist at y.' Yet, the fact that there is a time for each contingent entity at which it ceases to exist does not entail that there is one time at which all contingent entities cease to exist.

24   This demonstration seems to deny the possibility that every necessary entity is absolutely necessary, i.e., does not have its existence caused by another. The Third Way does not appear to offer any support for this principle, and certainly Aristotle—whose unmoved movers are necessary entities (see *Met* XII 7–8)—does not accept it. Be this as it may, Aquinas believes that pure actuality entails unicity (ST Ia.11.3c), thus as the subject of the Third Way is pure actuality (which it must be in order to function as an uncaused cause), it is the sole absolutely necessary entity.

25   Henceforth I no longer divide my treatment of each proof's status as scientific and analogical into two sections, supply formal reconstructions of each demonstration, or dwell at length on connections such as those between pure actuality and *per se* belonging.

26   For the demonstration that God is one, see ST Ia.11.3c; for the demonstration that God is the cause of the existence of all else, see ST Ia.44.1c. See also 'The First Way' above.

27   As noted in Chapter 1, whether Plato ever held this belief or perhaps held this belief and later rejected it is still an open question.

28   Cf. *Met* IX 10, 1051^{b}2–9, and ST Ia.16.2.

29   John Wippel, *The Metaphysical Thought of Thomas Aquinas: From Finite Being to Uncreated Being,* Monographs of the Society for Medieval and Renaissance Philosophy 1 (Washington, D.C.: The Catholic University of America Press, 2000), 471; see also ST Ia.16.1.

30   Wippel (n. 29), 471.

31   Pegis translates '*aliqui rei*' with 'some thing.' I have modified this translation, replacing his 'some thing' with 'anything.'

32   By 'noblest (*nobilissimum*)' Wippel believes that Aquinas means 'most perfect.' If he is correct, nobility itself should not be

looked on as a perfection, but rather an indication of the level of perfection possessed by the first being (see Wippel (n. 29), 472).

33 Pegis and the Fathers of the English Dominican Province translate '*scilicet*' with 'such as.' I have used 'namely' (also adopted by Kenny and Shanley), as Aquinas's Fifth Way considers only the end-directed activity of natural bodies. Cf., SCG III.24.4, where Aquinas clearly has in mind only natural bodies.

34 Kenny believes that Aquinas's 'things which lack intelligence' are things that lack consciousness: 'His starting point is the end-directedness of things which lack consciousness, which he calls "natural bodies": he means the lifeless elements and perhaps the plants and heavenly bodies' (Kenny (n. 4), 96–97). In his *History of Philosophy*, Frederick Copleston takes a narrower view: 'St. Thomas argues that we behold inorganic objects operating for an end' (Vol. 2, part 2, *Albert the Great to Duns Scotus*, 63). (Note, it is possible that Copleston changed his mind about this, for his later *Aquinas* merely has it that 'we observe material things of very different types cooperating in such a way as to produce and maintain a relatively stable world-order or system' [London: Penguin Books, 1955], 126.) Both commentators seem unnecessarily to limit the scope of Aquinas's 'natural bodies.' Aristotle's *On the Soul* (*An*) divides natural bodies into two groups, those that possess vitality and those that do not (*An* II 1, 412^{a}13). Vitality is a principle or cause through which an entity can nourish itself, grow, and decay (*An* II 1, 412^{a}14–15). This principle is the soul. The soul is 'actuality of the first kind of a natural organized body' (*An* II 1, 412^{b}5, trans. J. A. Smith). More simply, following Aquinas, the soul is 'that by which a living thing is alive' (*Sententia super De anima* (In DA), II.1, 220), or 'the actuality whereby the body has life' (ibid., 222). Types of souls are arranged in an order of increasing complexity, with the more complex souls comprising the powers of the less complex. The simplest soul is nutritive. Next in complexity is the sensitive soul. Combining the powers of these two and adding the capacity

for movement from place to place is the locomotive soul. Finally, the most complex soul is intellective (In DA II.3.225 = *An* II 2, 413^{a}11–413^{b}13). The Fifth Way's natural bodies lack the capacity for knowledge, but an entity can lack this capacity and yet be organic; insects for example possess motive souls (*An* II 2, 413^{b}19–21) while lacking intellective souls that would allow them the capacity for knowledge. Yet, insects are also of a higher level of complexity than plants, which possess only nutritive souls (*An* II 2, 413^{a}26–413^{b}1). Accordingly, there is no reason to limit the denotation of 'natural bodies' to Copleston's inorganic entities or Kenny's lifeless elements, plants, and entities possessing only nutritive souls. Again if Aquinas has such entities in mind this would strengthen his argument, for non-rational ensouled entities perform all sorts of functions that appear to be directed by a rational mind but, given an Aristotelian conception of a soul ordered with respect to powers, lack the rationality requisite for this behavior.

35   Cf. David Hume's *Dialogues Concerning Natural Religion*, part V.
36   Here Aquinas does not discuss the nature of providence, or whether God is constrained by the rationally optimal plan, but, at ST Ia.26.6, Aquinas appears to argue in favor of such a plan and assert that God cannot do otherwise than bring it to fruition.

4. Scotus and *Scientia*

1 For Scotus's distinction between degrees of certainty in relation to scientific knowledge as well as a discussion of its historical antecedents, see Eileen Serene, 'Demonstrative Science,' in CHLMP, 496–517.
2 On Aquinas's appraisal of the natural sciences, see Serene (n. 1), 504–7; on his belief in our ability to arrive at scientific knowledge of natural kinds, see Chapter 2 above.
3 See Edward Grant, 'The Effect of the Condemnation of 1277,' CHLMP, 537–39; and Serene (n. 1), 507–13.
4 As noted in Chapter 1, Steven Marrone has shown that Henry

moved away from this understanding later in his career ('Henry of Ghent and Duns Scotus on the Knowledge of Being,' *Speculum* 63, no. 1 (1988): 22–57). Yet even if Scotus is attacking a straw man, he is apparently unaware of the fact.

5 *Philosophical Writings*, 184, n. 27.

6 *Aristotle's 'Prior and Posterior Analytics'*, ed. Ross, 602.

7 The version of this proof that was known to Aristotle is that which later appears in Euclid's *Elements* as proposition 32. See Heath, ed., *The Thirteen Books of Euclid's 'Elements,'* vol. 1, 321.

5. Scotus on Naming and Understanding

1 *'Nullum nomen potest imponi alicui distinctius quam intelligatur'* (*Ord.* I, d. 22, q. un., n. 2., trans. mine). Cf. Aquinas, ST Ia.13.1c: 'We can give a name to anything in as far as we can understand it.'

2 'This widely accepted proposition—"as a thing is understood, so also it is named"—is false if literally understood [*ista proposito communis multis opinionibus—scilicet quod "sicut intelligitur, sic et nominatur"—falsa est si intelligatur praecise*]' (ibid., n. 4, trans. mine).

3 *'Dicitur quod sicut Deus intelligitur a nobis, ita potest et a nobis nominari. Secundum ergo quod diversimode aliqui sentiunt de cognitione Dei ab intellectu viatoris, ita consequenter dicunt diversimode de possibilitate etiam nominandi Deum,—et qui negat conceptum communem univocum Deo et creaturae et ponit duos conceptus analogos (quorum scilicet alter, qui est creaturae, attribuitur alteri, scilicet illi qui est Dei), dicet secundum hoc consequenter, quod Deus est nominabilis a viatore nomine exprimente illum conceptum analogum.'* Cf. *Ord.* I, d. 3, pars 1, q. 1, nn. 20–21. For Henry's statement of his position see his *Summa* 21.2, ad 3.

4 See *The Treatise on the Divine Nature*, trans. Shanley, 325–26.

5 See *Duns Scotus, Metaphysician*, ed. Frank and Wolter, 144; Edward Grant, 'The Effect of the Condemnation of 1277,' in CHLMP, 537–39; Eileen Serene, 'Demonstrative Science,' in CHLMP, 509; Zdzisław Kuksewicz, 'Criticisms of Aristotelian

Psychology and the Augustinian–Aristotelian Synthesis,' in CHLMP, 623–28; and Robert Pasnau, 'Cognition,' in Williams, *The Cambridge Companion to Duns Scotus*, 285–311.

6   *De Trinitate* 9.6. I discuss this passage in Chapter 1.

7   This discussion follows Frank and Wolter (n. 5), 140–44, see also *Ord.* I, d. 3, pars 1, q. 2, n. 21.

8   Frank and Wolter suggest that the claim that attributes we ascribe to God do not tell us anything of God's nature but rather something about (*circa*) that nature can be understood in terms of Bertrand Russell's distinction between knowledge by acquaintance and knowledge by description. Knowledge by acquaintance is about what we directly experience, whereas knowledge by description comes to us at one remove, e.g., through reports. Thus, to know what lies about God's essence is to know his effects without knowing the essence that produces these effects (see Frank and Wolter (n. 5), 141).

9   See note 3.

10 Citations from Appendix A provide the Vatican pagination as the material is not divided into enumerated paragraphs. '*Concedit enim viatorem habere aliquem conceptum quiditativum de Deo, et patet, quia alias nullum posset habere qualitativum nec relativum de ipso, nam conceptus qualitativus semper requirit aliquem quiditativum cui insit; sed secundum ipsum non potest haberi conceptus quiditativus de Deo, communis sibi et creaturae.*' Cf., *Ord.* I, d. 3, pars 1, q. 2, n. 25, 109: 'It is naturally possible to have not only a concept in which God is known incidentally, for example, in some attribute, but also some concept in which he is conceived *per se* and quidditatively. I prove this, because in conceiving "wise", we conceive a property, according to him [i.e., Henry], or a quasi-property, which perfects the nature as some further actuality. Hence in order to conceive "wise", it is necessary to think of some quiddity in which this quasi-property exists. And thus it is necessary to look beyond the ideas of all properties or quasi-properties to some quidditative concept to which we attribute these; and this concept will be a quidditative concept of God, because in no other sort will our quest cease' (*Duns Scotus, Metaphysician*, 109).

11 As for the relation that holds between creator and creation, it tells us something of God's essence inasmuch as he is the ground of this relation. However, God is not essentially (that is necessarily) a creator (*De primo princ.* 4.25). On the category of relation, see Peter King, 'Scotus on Metaphysics,' in Williams, *The Cambridge Companion to Duns Scotus*, 37.

12 '*Cum substantia non sit intelligibilis a viatore nisi in communi conceptu entis (sicut probatum est distinctione 3), si non possit distinctius significari quam intelligi, nullum nomen impositum a viatore significaret aliquam rem de genere substantiae.*'

13 '*Sicut praecise concipitur ab intellectu viatoris aliqua proprietas a qua imponitur nomen (quae proprietas communiter exprimitur per etymologiam nominis), ita praecise talis proprietas significaretur per nomen.*'

14 '*Ita potest argui de omnibus aliis nominibus, impositis rebus de genere substantiae, quod nullum illorum significat aliquid nisi proprietatem accidentalem aliquam quae intelligebatur ab imponente.*'

15 Literally: 'But they are not joined together in such a way in this whole as in that [whole].'

16 '*Concipiuntur ab aliquo multa accidentia, concurrentia in eodem, puta talis quantitas et talis qualitas ... Non autem coniunguntur talia in isto toto, qualia in illo: ex quo enim diversimode coniunguntur in diversis, concluditur substratum istis esse diversum a substrato illis, et ex hoc concluditur hoc esse aliud ab alio tertio. Sed isti alii, sic distincto ... imponitur nomen aliquod; illud videtur esse proprium signum "huius", sub ratione qua "hoc" est, ita quod imponens nomen, intendit illam significare, ita nomen quod imponit est signum, et tamen ipse non intelligit illud distincte, quod distincte intendit significare per hoc nomen vel hoc signum.*'

17 '*Nomina multa imponuntur quae significant Deum in communi, quia sic potest naturaliter concipi a viatore.*'

18 '*Est ... Deus nominabilis a viatore nomine significante proprie essentiam divinam ut est "haec essentia," quia viator potest uti illo signo et intendere exprimere significatum illius signi, sive ipse imposuerit illud signum sive alius quicumque qui cognovit significatum; et tali etiam signo vel nomine potest viator uti tamquam nomine, licet non potuerit illud imponere tamquam signum. Ut si illa propositio esset*

vera quod "nullum nomen potest imponi alicui distinctius quam intelligatur," haec tamen est falsa quod "nullus potest uti nomine, distinctius significante rem, quam ipse posit intelligere"; et ideo simpliciter concedendum est quod multis nominibus potest uti viator, exprimentibus essentiam divinam sub ratione essentiae divinae.'

19   Cf., *Quodl.* 14.13 where Scotus notes about transcendentals referred to the divine essence that: 'Any transcendent notion arrived at by abstraction from what is known of a creature can be thought of in its indifference [i.e., as common and unspecified] and in such a case God is conceived confusedly as it were, just as in thinking of animal, man is being thought of.'

20   '... *nomen quodcumque, significans aliquid quod huic soli potest inesse.'*

21   '*Sed simpliciter proprium nomen huius non est nisi quod primo significat hoc sub propria ratione, quia solum illud est proprium signum vocale huius.'*

22   Again note the parallelism in the account Scotus provides in his *Quaestiones Quodlibetales*, with respect to transcendentals predicated of God: 'If such a common transcendent concept is thought of as qualified by some more specific perfection such as supreme, first, or infinite, we obtain a concept which is proper to God in the sense that it is characteristic of no other being' (14.13).

23   '*Est igitur isto ordo: uti nomine ut tali re; ulterius, ut signo ad placitum alicuius, cuius tamen nullum conceptum habet utens (nisi in hoc universalissimo, quod est aliquid significatum hoc nomine); tertio, ut signo alicuius, cuius conceptum universalem tantum habet utens (intendit tamen exprimere illud quod significatur per nomen illud, licet illud sic in particulari non concipiat); quarto, ut signo expressivo proprii conceptus in particulari. Et hic semper gradus prior est imperfectus respectu posterioris: primis igitur est imperfectissimus, ultimus simpliciter perfectus.'*

24   An annotation in the *Ordinatio* (349–40) uses one of God's names to illustrate this type of language use. Scotus considers a Latin speaker putting together various Hebraic characters to form a Hebraic word whose signification he cannot grasp.

The word is composed of the four letters—'*jod*,' '*eth*,' '*vau*,' '*he*'—which together make the Tetragrammaton, a Hebraic name of God which, out of reverence, the Jewish community of believers ceased to pronounce sometime around the third century BC.

25 '*Vel habet conceptum … proprium … vel habet minus proprium seu confusum, utpote habens tantum conceptum animalis proferat hanc vocem "homo," intendens exprimere per nomen audienti illud quod alii concipiunt per nomen et ad quod est impositum, sciens ipsum esse impositum alicui speciei sub animali, quod tamen non intelligit in particulari sicut significatur per hoc nomen.*'

26 '*His praemissis, ad quaestionem sit prima conclusio haec: possible est Deum nomine simpliciter proprio nominari a viatore imperfecte, secundum tres gradus primos praedictos; secunda conclusio est haec: non est possible Deum perfecte nominari a viatore, scilicet secundum quartum gradum; tertia conclusio: qualiter de facto nominatur a nobis.*'

27 '*Nomen quodcumque est signum finitum, etiam si imponatur a Deo sibi secundum rationem immensitatis suae; ergo ad hoc ut sit alicui intelligenti signum, non oportet illum habere intellectionem infinitam. Potest igitur Deus quocumque nomine nominari ab intelligente finito.*'

28 '*Patet igitur quod alia est ratio a qua nomen imponitur (et illam significant etymologia), et alia cui imponitur; et ita licet imponens non habuerit conceptum distinctum nisi rationis, a qua imposuit nomen, non tamen imposuit nomen illi rationi, sed illi substantiae cuius est haec descriptio, et hoc sub propria ratione, quam tamen non sic intelligit,—et per consequens iste nominat ut imponens imperfecte secundum tertium gradum.*'

29 *Metaphysics*, III 3, 998^{b}21–26.

30 When different things are conceived through one of a term's significates (that is through one of the ideas that a term brings to mind), those things are univocated by that term (Giorgio Pini, *Categories and Logic in Duns Scotus: An Interpretation of Aristotle's "Categories" in the Later Thirteenth Century* [Leiden: Brill, 2002], 173).

6. Scotus on the Signification of Theological Discourse

1   See *Quaestiones in librum Praedicamentorum*, q. 4, n. 32; Marmo, 'A Pragmatic Approach to Language in Modism,' 169–83; and Ashworth's "Analogy and Equivocation in Thirteenth-Century Logic," 94–135.

2   See also Richard Cross, 'Where Angels Fear to Tread,' *Antonianum* 76 (2001): 7–41; Thomas Williams, 'The Doctrine of Univocity is True and Salutary,' *Modern Theology* 21, no. 4 (2005): 575–85; James Ross and Todd Bates, 'Duns Scotus on Natural Theology,' in Williams, *The Cambridge Companion to Duns Scotus*, 193–237.

3   This appraisal of the difficulties Scotus must navigate and the subsequent discussion of his resolution follows Peter King's 'Scotus on Metaphysics,' in Williams, *The Cambridge Companion to Duns Scotus*, 15–68.

4   Scotus allows that accidents are in principle separable from substances as in the sacrament of the Eucharist, where the accidents of bread and wine remain after their transubstantiation. See, King (n. 3), 28–30; Scotus, *Philosophical Writings*, 165–68, nn. 2–5; and *Duns Scotus, Metaphysician*, ed. Frank and Wolter, 159–64.

5   This is indicated in a marginal note found in three manuscripts of his revised *Ordinatio* (Frank and Wolter (n. 4), 180, n. 37).

6   Stephen Dumont, 'Transcendental Being: Scotus and Scotists,' *Topoi* 11, no. 2 (1992): 137.

7   Ross translates Aristotle's 'ἕτερον' with 'other.' I replace 'other' with 'diverse' and alter the prepositions as needed, in this way adjusting for the translation of '*diversum*' with 'diverse.'

8   See King (n. 3), 20.

9   '*Quomodo potest conceptus communis Deo et creaturae "realis" accipi, nisi ab aliqua realitate eiusdem generis, —et tunc videtur quod sit potentialis ad illam realitatem a qua accipitur conceptus distinguens … Si esset aliqua realitas distinguens in re, et alia distincta, videtur quod res sit composita, quia habet aliquid quo conveniat et quo differat.*' Within an individual thing, the concept of genus and difference are formally as opposed to really distinct.

The formal distinction distinguishes between *rationes* (descriptions that pick out features that belong to something) that are existentially inseparable, on the grounds that 'existential inseparability does not entail identity in definition' (King (n. 3), 22). Thus one can find various ways of describing an entity without committing to the 'full-blooded' existence of that about which one speaks (ibid., 21). This accounts for the odd sounding locution 'some reality of its genus.' What Scotus means by this is simply 'some genus that subsumes both God and creatures,' but owing to his belief that genera and specific differences are only formally distinct within an individual he describes this hypothetical common genus as 'some reality [*aliqua realitate*].' Note though that outside of an individual, genera and specific differences are really as opposed to formally distinct (ibid., n. 26).

10   '*Quando intelligitur aliqua realitas cum modo suo intrinseco, ille conceptus non est ita simpliciter simplex quin possit concipi illa realitas absque modo illo, sed tunc est conceptus imperfectus illius rei; potest etiam concipi sub illo modo, et tunc est conceptus perfectus illius rei. Exemplum: si esset albedo in decimo gradu intensionis, quantumcumque esset simplex omni modo in re, posset tamen concipi sub ratione albedinis tantae, et tunc perfecte conciperetur conceptu adaequato ipsi rei,—vel posset concipi praecise sub ratione albedinis, et tunc conciperetur conceptu imperfecto et deficiente a perfectione rei; conceptus autem imperfectus posset esse communis albedini illi et alii, et conceptus perfectus proprius esset.*

     Requiritur ergo distinctio, inter illud a quo accipitur conceptus communis et inter illud a quo accipitur conceptus proprius, non ut distinctio realitatis et realitatis sed ut distinctio realitatis et modi proprii et intrinseci eiusdem,—quae distinctio sufficit ad habendum conceptum perfectum vel imperfectum de eodem, quorum imperfectum sit communis et perfectus sit proprius. Sed conceptus generis et differentiae requirunt distinctionem realitatum, non tantum eiusdem realitatis perfecte et imperfecte conceptae.'

11   King (n. 3), 18–21.

7. Infinitude, Transcendental Signification and Analogy

1 See James Ross and Todd Bates, 'Duns Scotus on Natural Theology', in Williams, *The Cambridge Companion to Duns Scotus*, 212–13.

2 Though identical with his essence, God's perfections and attributes are formally distinct from one another. That is, there is a real difference between these traits such that they are definable without reference to one another. God's attributes are nonetheless inseparable from one another, even through divine agency (ibid., 211–12). Now in creatures, the formal distinction implies some sort of composition since formally distinct aspects of one and the same thing perfect one another, as with human beings rationality perfects animality. Yet, all of God's traits are present in the highest degree possible, and so cannot perfect one another. As his traits do not stand in this relation of potentiality to one another, when the formal distinction is applied to God it implies even less composition than when it is used with reference to creatures (see *John Duns Scotus: God and Creatures; The Quodlibetal Questions*, trans. with intro, notes and glossary by Felix Alluntis and Allan Wolter [Washington, D.C.: The Catholic University of America Press, 1975], Glossary, s.vv. 'Formal Distinction,' 'Formal Predication,' 'Formality;' and Peter King, 'Scotus on Metaphysics', in Williams, *The Cambridge Companion to Duns Scotus*, esp. 25–28).

3 Constantino Marmo uses a similar analogy to describe Scotus's understanding of the formal distinction, which Scotus uses to distinguish conceptually distinct elements (or formalities) within one and the same individual ('Ontology and Semantics in the Logic of Duns Scotus,' in *On the Medieval Theory of Signs*, edited by Umberto Eco and Constantino Marmo, Foundations of Semiotics 21, edited by Achim Eschbach [Philadelphia: John Benjamins Publishing Company, 1989], 159). Marmo draws this analogy from Eberhard Wölfel, '*Seinsstruktur und Trinitätsproblem: Untersuchungen zur Grundlegung der natürlichen Theologie bei Johannes Duns Scotus* (Münster: Aschendorff, 1965), 40.

4 See Robert Pasnau, 'Cognition,' in Williams, *The Cambridge Companion to Duns Scotus*, 285–311; and *John Duns Scotus, God*

and *Creatures: The Quodlibetal Questions*, ed. Alluntis and Wolter, Glossary, s.v. 'Intelligible Species.'

5 This precedes his demonstration of God's infinitude. But, as we shall see when discussing Scotus's *Quodlibetal Questions*, God's possession of every perfection is dependent on his infinitude.

6 See Thomas Williams, *The Cambridge Companion to Duns Scotus*, Introduction.

7 Compare Catherine Pickstock's assessment: 'The univocity of Being between God and creature paradoxically gives rise to a kind of equivocity, for the difference of degree or amount of Being disallows any specific resemblance between them, and excludes the possibility of figural or analogical determinations of God that give us any degree of substantive knowledge of His character. By withdrawing the means through which creatures might distinguish themselves ontologically from God through figuring or analogically drawing near Him, the distance between the infinite and the finite becomes an undifferentiated and *quantified* (although unquantifiable) abyss. Thus, the "same" becomes the radically disparate and unknowable' (Pickstock, *After Writing*, 123). In support of the claim that Scotus's work lends itself to a conception of God as radically disparate and unknowable Pickstock cites *De primo principio* 4.86. The passage reads: 'Besides the aforesaid points which the philosophers have affirmed of you, Catholics often praise you as omnipotent, immense, omnipresent, just yet merciful, provident of all creatures but looking after intellectual ones in a special way, but these matters are deferred to the next tract. In this first treatise I have tried to show how the metaphysical attributes affirmed of you can be inferred in some way by natural reason [*ratione naturali*]. In the tract which follows, those shall be set forth that are the subject of belief, wherein reason is held captive—yet to Catholics, the latter are the more certain since they rest firmly upon your own most solid truth and not upon our intellect which is blind and weak in many things.' This passage acknowledges that several perfections inhere in the divine essence, claims that the entire treatise has been a demonstration of the power of unaided reason to learn of the divine essence, and

notes that in his next work Scotus will discuss truths of faith which lie beyond the discernment of reason (this next work may be the so-called *tractatus de creditis*, whether the work is Scotus's is still debated (see Williams, *The Cambridge Companion to Scotus*, Introduction)). Moreover, in the passages immediately preceding this Scotus claims to have demonstrated that (among other things) God is the first efficient cause, the ultimate end, supreme in perfection, transcending all things, uncaused in any way, incapable of becoming or perishing, and necessarily existent (4.84–85). Now Scotus does claim that figurative or analogical discourse cannot provide substantive knowledge of God's essence, but this is owing to rejection of modist semantics. This belief need not be attended with a confession that we lack knowledge of God's essence. Thus however Scotus is received, he would reject the claim that God is 'radically disparate and unknowable.'

Index

accidents (capacity to move
intellect) 93–5, 98–9 *see also
under* categories; *per se*
actuality-potentiality *see under* Five
Ways: God
analogy
of attribution 13–15, 26, 48–9,
51–2, 54, 56–9, 67, 72–3, 101,
120 (*see also under* Five Ways)
and *scientia* (*see under* Five Ways)
and Scotus (*see* Henry of Ghent:
analogy; Modistae)
An.Post I 4, 73ᵇ, 16–18, 32–9
apophatic theology 6, 11–12, 16,
51–2, 57, 115
Aristotle, transmission and
reception of 2–5, 13–14, 20,
133n. 11
articles of faith 3
arts, faculty of 3, 5, 6, 133n. 11
Augustine 2, 4–5, 18, 68, 89
Averroes 4, 6, 133n. 15

Barnes, Jonathan 33
being *see* categories; univocity
Boethius 14
Burrell, David 134n. 28

categories 20–2, 103, 105–6
cause *see under* Five Ways; *per se*;
scientia
concepts *see under* signification;
terms; transcendentals

Condemnation of 1277 3–5, 7, 18,
75, 89
contingency-necessity *see under* Five
Ways; *scientia*
Copleston, Frederick 155n. 34

definition *see under scientia*
demonstration *see under* Five Ways;
scientia
difference and diversity 102, 105,
106–7
Dionysius (Pseudo) 10–11, 68,
137n. 40
distinction
formal 111–12, 136n. 38,
162n. 2
modal 107–8, 118
real 107–8, 136n. 38
see also realities (*realitates*)

epistemic access, four levels
(Scotus) 88, 93, 96–9

faith and reason 1–3, 7, 115,
131nn. 1–2
Five Ways
analogy and *scientia* in
First Way 55–9
Second Way 63–4
Third Way 66
Fourth Way 69–71
Fifth Way 72–3
and analogy of attribution (in

general) 26, 48–50, 56–8, 67,
    73
contingency-necessity 51, 56, 59,
    65–6
exemplar causality 51, 68–9
God
    first efficient cause 60, 62–4
    per se existent 55–6, 59, 63, 66,
        72, 152n. 16
    possession of every perfection
        51–2, 70, 73
    pure activity of 49–51, 55–9,
        63–7, 70–3
    as reflexive *per se* cause 49,
        56–8
    of revelation 53, 70
    supreme governor 71–2
    uncaused 49, 54, 56, 65
    unmoved mover 55–9
    per se vs. *per accidens* series 60–3
    as scientific demonstrations (in
        general) 49–57, 66–7, 73,
        150n. 6
formal distinction *see under*
    distinction
forms *see under* Plato

Gilson, Etienne 15

Henry of Ghent
    analogy 17–20, 73, 87–92, 120
    fivefold ascent to knowledge of
        God 89–90
    illumination 2–6, 9, 17–19, 75–6,
        89–92
    negatively vs. primatively
        indeterminate concepts 89,
        92

Ibn Rushd 4, 6, 133n. 15
ideas *see under* signification; terms
illumination *see under* Henry of
    Ghent

imposition 23, 73, 86, 93–5, 99
infinitude
    delimits knowledge of God
        10–13, 24–6, 74, 85, 99–100,
        104, 109, 110–20
    quantitatively infinite in act 116–18
    see also under signification;
        transcendentals
inherence *see under per se*
Isidore of Seville 94

James of Venice 36–7, 145n. 7
John of Salisbury 37, 145n. 7
John XXI (Pope) 4
Jordan, Mark 131n. 2

Kenny, Anthony 147n. 18, 155n. 34
knowledge *see under* epistemic access;
        infinitude theology; *scientia*;
        transcendentals; univocity

Latin Averroism 4, 6, 133n. 15

Marmo, Constantino 140n. 55,
        164n. 3
modal distinction *see under*
    distinction
Modistae 23, 73, 140n. 55, 165n. 7

natural theology
    Aquinas 1, 3–5, 7, 9, 10, 48, 56–7,
        67, 73, 88, 111
    defined 2, 6
    Scotus 4–9, 25, 73, 84–8, 105,
        111–14
    see also under signification
necessity-contingency *see under* Five
        Ways; *scientia*
negative theology 6, 11–12, 16,
        51–2, 57, 115

per se
    accident (property)

in conclusion of scientific
   demonstration 35, 37–9, 41,
   45–8 (*see also under Five Ways*)
counterpredicable 39
defined 30–2, 34, 39, 91–2
and *scientia* (at *An.Post* I 4, 73^b
   16–18) 32–9
belonging
   and Aristotle's four causes 29–32
   defined 29, 148n. 20
cause (defined) 30, 49
ordered series 60–3
see also under scientia
philosophy and theology 1–3, 7,
   115, 131nn. 1–2
Pickstock, Catherine 134n. 28,
   143n. 69, 151n. 13, 165n. 7
Plato
   medieveal Platonism 2, 10, 13,
      68–70
   theory of forms 9–10, 13, 68
potentiality-actuality
   see under Five Ways: God
predicaments 20–2, 103, 105–6
predication *see under* analogy;
      scientia; signification; terms;
      univocity
propter quid see under scienrta
Pseudo-Dionysius 10–11, 68, 137n. 40

quia see under scientia

real distinction *see under* distinction
realities (*realitates*) 107–9, 162n. 9
reflexive causality 49, 56–8
Richard of Conington 18
Ross, W. D. 33

Scholasticism 1–2
scientia
   apodictic vs. probable (Scotus)
      75, 77–80, 82–4
   defined 39–40, 83

and definition (nominal-real)
   in the Five Ways 49–51, 56, 63
   in general 29–30, 40–1, 44
demonstration (scientific)
middle (as cause) 29, 40–7, 49
propter quid-quia 42–5, 50
schematism of scientific syllogism
   28, 38, 41, 45, 55
vs. *intellectus* and *cognitio* 38
of natural kinds 28, 41, 49, 75
necessary 28, 30, 34, 38–41, 46,
   48–50, 75, 147n. 18
and *per se* belonging
   in the Five Ways 55–6, 63, 66, 72
   in general 29–33, 37–8, 41–2,
      45–7
principles (causes) of 38, 40, 42,
   80, 81, 148n. 20
principle of regularity of nature
   (Scotus) 75, 79–80, 83–4
see *also under* Five Ways; *per se*
Siger of Brabant 3–6
signification
   direct vs. indirect 8–9
   naming follows understanding
      86–99
   prior and posterior 14, 22–4, 73,
      101, 120
   theological discourse
      Aquinas 7, 10–17, 26, 48, 51,
         58, 67, 73–4, 100–1, 120
      Scotus 7, 13, 16–17, 20, 22–6,
         73–4, 84–7, 94–106, 109–11,
         114, 120
      see also under transcendentals;
         univocity
Stephen Tempier 4, 17
substance *see* accidents (capacity to
      move intellect)

terms
   imposition of 23, 73, 86, 93–5, 99
   univocating 17, 20, 100

see also under analogy;
 signification; univocity
theology and philosophy 1–3, 7,
 115, 131nn. 1–2
transcendentals
 acquired via abstraction 103,
  120
 defined 10–12, 102
 infinitude, regulative function of
  21–2, 24–6, 85, 99–100, 104,
  109–10, 114, 120
 univocal though not proper to
  both God and creatures 22,
  24, 26, 74, 101, 109, 114
 see also under signification;
  univocity
Tredennick, Hugh 33–4
Trinity 112–13, 116

truth, ontological vs. logical
 (Aquinas) 68–9

univocity
 of being 20, 23, 103–8
 defined 7, 16–17, 105
 in theological discourse 7, 16–17,
  20, 22–4, 26, 73–4, 103–9, 120
 see also under signification;
  transcendentals

via negativa
 see under apophatic theology

William of Moerbeke 37, 145n.7
Williams, Thomas 151n. 13
Wippel, John 139n. 47
Wolter, Allen 134n. 28

Lightning Source UK Ltd.
Milton Keynes UK
UKOW032242050713

213333UK00001B/14/P